The Complete ESL/EFL Cooperative & Communicative Activity Book

Stephen Sloan

National Textbook Company

NTC a division of *NTC Publishing Group* • Lincolnwood, Illinois USA

About the Author

Stephen Sloan is an advisor in the Office of Bilingual ESL Instruction for the Los Angeles Unified School District. After many years with CATESOL, he served as the 1990–91 president. In addition, he works with adult-school teachers in Los Angeles.

Stephen Sloan has been a classroom teacher for over twenty years, with extensive experience with junior- and senior-high-school ESL students at all levels.

1992 Printing

Published by National Textbook Company, a division of NTC Publishing Group.
©1991 by NTC Publishing Group, 4255 West Touhy Avenue,
Lincolnwood (Chicago), Illinois 60646-1975 U.S.A.
Manufactured in the United States of America.

2 3 4 5 6 7 8 9 VP 9 8 7 6 5 4 3 2

Contents

Match-Ups 73

Part Three: Jigsaw Activities 115

Introduction

The Complete ESL/EFL Cooperative and Communicative Activity Book is a black-line master book of learner-directed activities for the intermediate-level English classroom. The activities are divided into three sections: strip stories, interviews and match-ups, and jigsaw activities.

In a strip story activity, each student in a cooperative learning group is given one or more segments of a story. The group members must work together to re-create the story. In order to do this, the students need to understand their parts of the story and the total story in such a way that they can communicate their understanding to the rest of the group.

Interviews and match-ups both require students to circulate among their classmates seeking information. An interview is a kind of treasure hunt and ice-breaker combined, in which students ask questions, listen to their classmates' answers, and obtain signatures from classmates with the "correct" answers. In a match-up, each student must find a classmate who holds an information card that in some way matches or complements his or her own card. The entire class then "approves" the matches.

Jigsaw activities require groups of students to cooperate in problem-solving. Each member of a group has a piece of information to share with the rest of the group. The students are not allowed to show their information to the others in their group. Instead, they must read or paraphrase the information out loud for the group.

Each type of activity involves a different kind of communication. This is not a grammar instruction book. It is a communication practice book. The goal of each activity is for students to use the language they have learned or acquired in a setting that is less controlled than structured practice but less random than unstructured conversation.

Understanding Cooperative Learning

Much of the methodology used in this book is based upon the concepts of cooperative learning espoused by Dr. Spencer Kagan, Dr. Mike Auer, and others. Cooperative learning is a set of teaching strategies that puts the learner in the center of the learning process. It equips the learner with whatever he or she needs to be a functioning member of a work group and then assigns tasks to the group that are both engaging and meaningful.

In cooperative learning, the basic work group is composed of four students. For best results, the group members should be carefully selected by the teacher to include students of varying abilities. For example, a top student could work with a bottom student and two students of average ability. This type of grouping has been found to encourage communication and to stimulate all of the students to interact.

No additional knowledge of cooperative learning strategies is needed to succeed in using the activities in this book. However, many fine books on cooperative learning strategies are available for teachers who wish to explore this approach to classroom learning in more detail.

Using Strip Stories

Part One of this book contains ten strip story units. The procedure for using a strip story is simply to duplicate and cut apart one copy of the story per group. (Each strip story is divided into either eight or twelve segments to be distributed equally among the participants. Cooperative learning groups of four can be combined to make circles of eight or twelve students to accommodate the story. Usually there will be one strip per student.) The group members must work together to re-create the story. The students are not permitted to show their strips to the rest of their group, so they must read or paraphrase their strips out loud. To increase the challenge for a more advanced class, the students can be given two minutes to memorize their strips and then turn them in before the groups begin to assemble their stories. The group members may use any methods they choose to assemble their story. Developing strategies for cooperating to achieve a goal is one of the purposes of this type of activity.

After each group has completed its story, the groups should be given a chance to tell or read their stories to the class. Part of the fun is to see how each group has put the story together. There is not always a single correct way to put together a story, but the class must agree that each version makes sense or else suggest appropriate changes. The class should discuss the reasons why certain orderings of the story "work" and others don't. These reasons may involve details of both syntax and semantics.

Each strip story unit includes a strip narrative with comprehension questions and a strip dialog with comprehension questions. These "Questions for Understanding" may be used to check students' comprehension of the story and may lead to a more detailed examination of certain cultural topics or linguistic structures relevant to the story. In addition, each unit contains several discussion/composition questions and some suggested activities. The "Questions for Discussion and Composition" provide a basis for oral or written discussions of American culture and comparisons of American culture to the students' native cultures. The "Activities" can be assigned to individuals, small groups, or the whole class to encourage students to extend and/or personalize the unit topics. The activities may lead students to attend a school sports event or interview the principal about his or her college experiences. Reports on these experiences may take the form of taped "radio commercials" or graphs and charts. The primary goal of the activities is to give students the opportunity to use English in new and different ways.

Using Interviews and Match-Ups

Interviews. Part Two of this book contains ten interviews. An interview is a one-page activity that provides an interesting way for students to get out of their seats and get to know their classmates better. Each interview sheet asks students to find people who meet certain criteria (e.g., have plaid shorts, can swim, or have never climbed a tree). The students must try to find classmates who meet these criteria, being careful to notice whether the interview sheet requires a positive or a negative response. When "interviewing" their classmates, the students should be instructed to use complete question forms that correspond to the answers sought (e.g., "Will you have finished your homework by 6:00 tonight?"). Through asking and answering questions, the students learn about each other's backgrounds and interests. The interviews also provide practice in using specific verb tenses and other grammatical structures.

Before class, the teacher must make one copy of the interview sheet for each student in the class. At class time, the interview sheets are distributed and the students are instructed to move around the classroom and find people who qualify to sign each line of their interview sheet. The goal is to fill the sheet with signatures. Unless the class is extremely small, no student should sign a classmate's paper more than once. It is possible that no one in the class will qualify to sign a particular line of the paper. When this occurs, the teacher may extend the activity by having students interview people outside of class to try to fill their sheets. However, penalizing students for not filling their sheets is discouraged.

After the students have finished getting signatures, the class should discuss the process of conducting the interviews. When appropriate, this discussion can include reasons why it was difficult to find someone to sign a particular line.

Match-Ups. Part Two also contains nine match-ups. In a match-up activity, students are given information on individual cards. Each card has a "matching" card that contains missing or complementary information. The students circulate among their classmates to try to find their partners. Whenever possible, the students should be encouraged to give information about themselves or their cards rather than ask questions. They are not allowed to show their cards to anyone until they think they have found their correct partners. Depending on the level of the class, the teacher may wish to have the students use a very simple matching process (e.g., I'm *gone*. I'm the past participle of *go*) or a more challenging procedure, such as using their verb in a sentence and listening to each other's sentences to identify their partner.

As the partners find each other, they should move to a designated area of the room. When all the students have paired up, the pairs take turns reading their cards aloud. The class then approves or disapproves the matches. If any pairs are matched incorrectly, the class should work together to correct the matches.

Before using a match-up activity, the teacher simply needs to make one copy of each page containing information cards for the activity and cut apart the cards. Match-ups can easily be adapted to any class size by removing (or, if a class is extremely large, adding) pairs of cards to achieve a total of one card per student.

For classes with an odd number of students, the teacher should take a card and participate in the activity.

Several of the match-ups are supplemented by crossword puzzles that reinforce the language used in the match-up activity. These crossword puzzles may be duplicated and distributed for use in class or as homework assignments.

Using Jigsaw Activities

Part Three contains five jigsaw activities, classic cooperative learning activities that require groups of students to cooperate in solving some kind of problem or achieving some kind of goal. Each activity contains a detailed "Directions to the Teacher" section, plus a student direction page, one or more information pages, and a solution page. Each cooperative learning group receives one copy of everything except the directions to the teacher. (In some cases, the information pages must be cut apart before being distributed.)

For each activity, the students are instructed to read the directions and ask any questions they may have about the procedure. Then they must work in their groups to solve the problem, recording their solution in a specific manner on the appropriate page (e.g., a check register or a family tree). When all the groups are finished, they should take turns sharing their results with the class. The class can then discuss any variations among the results and the different reasons and procedures used to reach those results.

Teaching with This Book

The activities in this book may be used in any order that complements the other instructional materials being used in a class. For convenient record-keeping, a checklist of the activities is provided on page 7. Instructors can make a copy of this checklist for each of their classes and use it to record the date each activity was used, along with any comments about the activity.

The activities range in length from thirty or forty minutes to a whole week of class time. For example, a strip story generally takes about forty-five minutes to complete. However, a strip story unit can take an entire week if all the accompanying questions and activities are used. The narrative strip story and comprehension questions may be used during one class period; the dialog strip story and comprehension questions may be used during the next class period; and the discussion/composition questions and activities may take one to three class periods as well as some student preparation outside of class.

The interviews generally take thirty to forty minutes to complete, although they can generate lengthy discussions based on any unusual answers. Interviews are excellent activities for the beginning of the semester because they get students talking to each other. Using a couple of interviews per week at the beginning of the semester and then one a week after that will keep the class alert and interested. Match-ups also take about thirty minutes, but additional class time may be required if the class has to correct several inappropriate matches. The crossword puzzles may be used as homework or as individual follow-up.

Jigsaw activities usually take one or two whole class periods. The first activity will likely take the longest, as the students become used to working in groups and learn how to engage all the members of the group. Using one activity approximately every other week will spread these enjoyable and productive sessions throughout the semester.

This book of black-line masters contains everything (except scissors, tape, and a photocopy machine!) that is needed to conduct engaging, communicative activities in the English-language classroom. In each activity, the teacher should strive to keep teaching to a minimum. The teacher's role is that of facilitator and clarifier. As the students complete the activities, they should be encouraged to try to solve as many of their own problems as possible. The teacher should only offer advice or answer a student's question if no one in the student's work group can answer the question. Even then, it is better to give a hint than a direct answer. The students will work harder to communicate with each other if they are the source of the answers.

The activities in this book contain messages of American culture and also a hint of American humor. This is intentional. Above all, human communication should be joyful. These language activities should be a joy to the students, not a drudgery. At the same time, this book is designed to aid teachers by providing easy-to-use, successful, and enjoyable activities that promote cooperation and communicative competence in English.

Acknowledgments

I thought this book would be my first one written alone. I was wrong — you can't do it alone. I would like to express my thanks to the following people: to the many students who have participated in the activities that make up this book; to my colleagues at Hollywood Community Adult School and the Office of Bilingual ESL Instruction who have offered superb assistance; to my wife, Maureen, who as always has supported me with love and provided expertise as a teacher; and to Kathleen Schultz of National Textbook Company who has been a wonderful help and a patient advisor.

Teacher's Checklist

Class _____

Term _____

Activity	Date	Comments
Strip Stories		
1. Cheerleaders		
2. Dating		
3. Teachers		
4. Car Troubles		
5. City Transportation		
6. A Birthday Party		
7. Before the Soccer Match		
8. Social Life		
9. Buying Music		
10. Holiday Shopping		
Interviews		
1. Ownership		
2. Everyday Actions		
3. Things People Can and Can't Do		
4. Things People Did and Didn't Do		
5. Things People Will and Won't Do		
6. Things People Have Done		
7. Things People Haven't Done		
8. Things Pairs of People Have and Haven't Done		
9. Things People Will Have Done		
10. Movie Survey		

Teacher's Checklist

Class _____

Term _____

Activity	Date	Comments
Match-Ups		
1. What Am I?		
Crossword Puzzle		
2. Participle Match-Up		
Crossword Puzzle		
3. Around the House Match-Up		
Crossword Puzzle		
4. Occupation Match-Up		
Crossword Puzzle		
5. Greeting Card Match-Up		
Crossword Puzzle		
6. Geography Match-Up		
Crossword Puzzle		
7. Meal Match-Up		
Crossword Puzzle		
8. Party Un-Mixer		
9. Dicto-Pictures		
Jigsaw Activities		
1. Making a Family Budget		
2. Going to Treasure Island		
3. Lower Wages for Youths		
4. Reporting a Crime		
5. Building a Family Tree		

The Complete ESL/EFL Cooperative and Communicative Activity Book

Part

1

Strip
Stories

1. Cheerleaders

Narrative

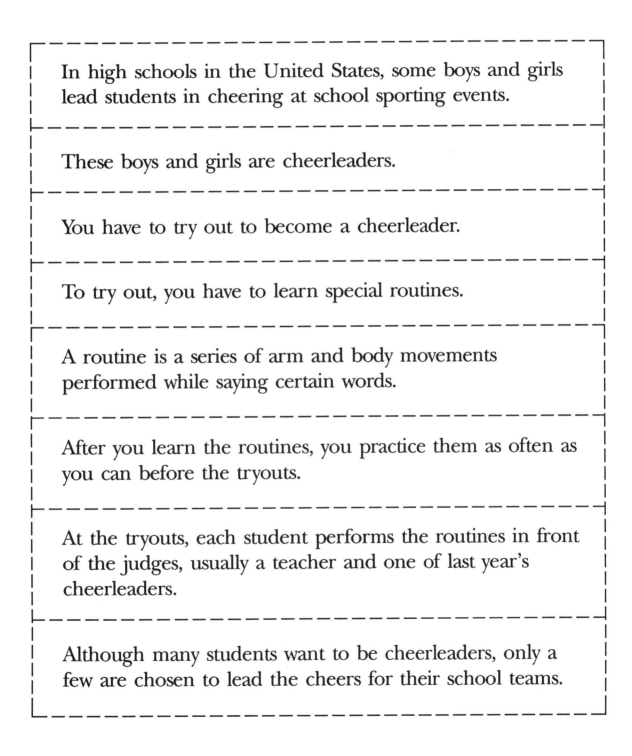

In high schools in the United States, some boys and girls lead students in cheering at school sporting events.

These boys and girls are cheerleaders.

You have to try out to become a cheerleader.

To try out, you have to learn special routines.

A routine is a series of arm and body movements performed while saying certain words.

After you learn the routines, you practice them as often as you can before the tryouts.

At the tryouts, each student performs the routines in front of the judges, usually a teacher and one of last year's cheerleaders.

Although many students want to be cheerleaders, only a few are chosen to lead the cheers for their school teams.

Questions for Understanding

Ask the students these questions.

1. What do cheerleaders do?
2. How do you become a cheerleader?
3. What age are cheerleaders?

1. Cheerleaders

Dialog

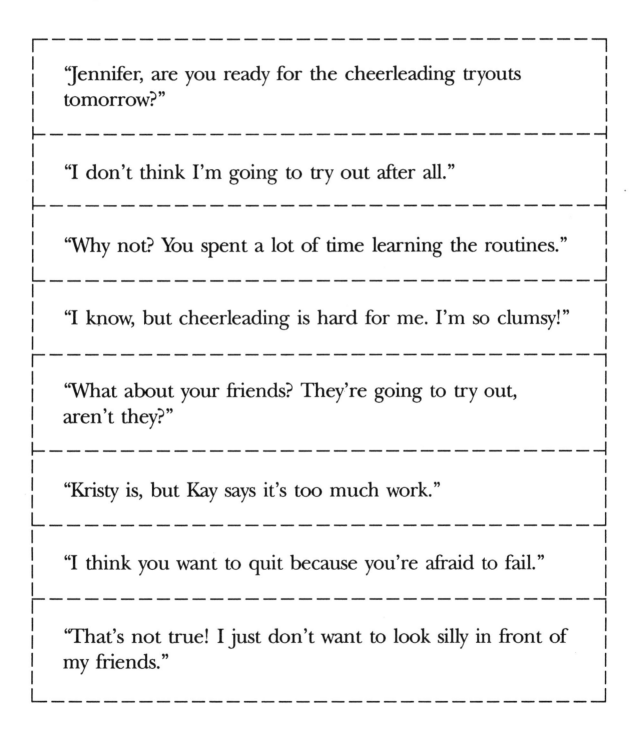

"Jennifer, are you ready for the cheerleading tryouts tomorrow?"

"I don't think I'm going to try out after all."

"Why not? You spent a lot of time learning the routines."

"I know, but cheerleading is hard for me. I'm so clumsy!"

"What about your friends? They're going to try out, aren't they?"

"Kristy is, but Kay says it's too much work."

"I think you want to quit because you're afraid to fail."

"That's not true! I just don't want to look silly in front of my friends."

Questions for Understanding

Ask the students these questions.

1. What was Jennifer planning to do?
2. In your opinion, who is talking to Jennifer?
3. Are Jennifer's friends going to try out?
4. Why does Jennifer want to quit?

Questions for Discussion and Composition

Present these questions as a basis for class discussions or writing assignments.

1. How do students in other countries show school spirit?
2. What kind of person would make a good cheerleader?
3. Does cheering really help a team to win?

Activities

Assign these activities to individuals, small groups, or the whole class to reinforce and expand on the lesson topic.

1. Learn and demonstrate a cheer for one of your school's sports teams.
2. Make up and demonstrate a cheer for your class or group.
3. Go to a school sports event and join in the cheering.

2. Dating

Narrative

American high school students often go out on dates.

Boys usually ask girls for dates, but sometimes girls ask boys out.

Teenagers often go on double dates. Two couples, two boys and two girls, go out together.

Friday and Saturday evenings are the most common times for dates.

Movies, parties, and school dances are popular places to go on dates.

Most teenagers' parents like to meet their child's date before the teens go out.

Parents usually tell the young people what time they must be home from their date.

For most American teenagers, dating is a fun part of growing up.

Questions for Understanding

Ask the students these questions.

1. What is double-dating?
2. When and where do teenagers usually go on dates?
3. What part do parents usually play in dating?

2. Dating

Dialog

"Hello, Nancy, this is Robert. I'm in your history class."

"Hi, Robert. I know who you are."

"I'm sorry I didn't get a chance to talk to you at school today."

"Oh, really? Did you want to tell me something?"

"Actually, I wanted to ask if you would go to the school dance with me on Friday."

"I'd like to go, Robert, but my parents won't let me single-date."

"That's O.K. We could go with Rick Hersh and Jeanie Mendoza. You know them, don't you?"

"I know Rick. He's in my English class, and my parents know his parents."

"Great! Can we pick you up at 7:30 on Friday? The dance starts at 8:00."

"That's fine, but I think my mother would like to meet you first."

"No problem. Why don't I drive you home from school tomorrow? I can meet her then."

"That sounds good. Thanks for calling, Robert. I'll see you tomorrow in class."

Questions for Understanding

Ask the students these questions.

1. Why is Robert calling Nancy?
2. When is the school dance?
3. What must Robert do before the dance?
4. Who are Rick Hersh and Jeanie Mendoza?

Questions for Discussion and Composition

Present these questions as a basis for class discussions or writing assignments.

1. At what age should young people begin to date?
2. What purpose does dating serve?
3. In what ways should parents be involved in their children's dating?

Activities

Assign these activities to individuals, small groups, or the whole class to reinforce and expand on the lesson topic.

1. Make a list of good places to go on a date.
2. Make a list of dating rules that teenagers should follow.
3. Conduct a survey among the students in your school to determine the favorite place to go on a date. Make a graph to show the results of your survey.

3. Teachers

Narrative

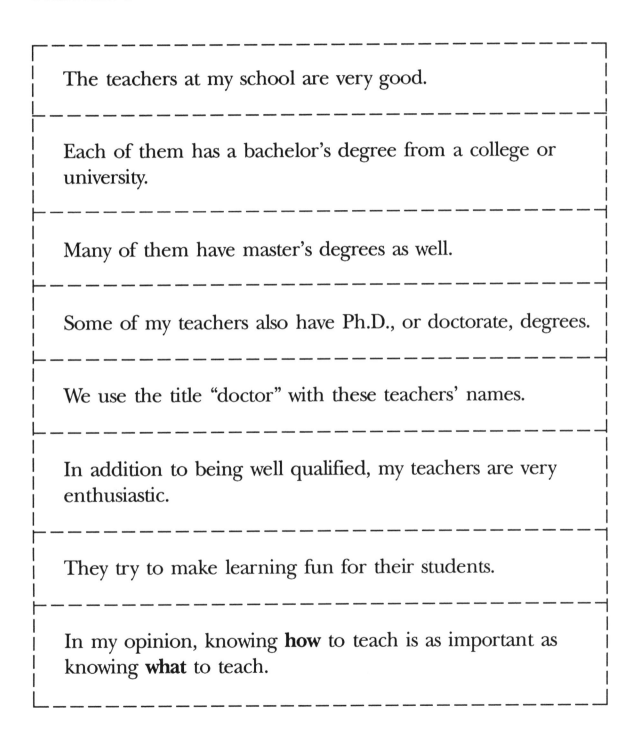

The teachers at my school are very good.

Each of them has a bachelor's degree from a college or university.

Many of them have master's degrees as well.

Some of my teachers also have Ph.D., or doctorate, degrees.

We use the title "doctor" with these teachers' names.

In addition to being well qualified, my teachers are very enthusiastic.

They try to make learning fun for their students.

In my opinion, knowing **how** to teach is as important as knowing **what** to teach.

Questions for Understanding

Ask the students these questions. (The answers to the starred questions are not provided in the narrative.)

1. What do you know about the author of this narrative?
2. Do these teachers know a lot about the subjects they teach? How do you know?
3. What do you call a person who has a Ph.D. degree?
*4. What is a bachelor's degree?
*5. What is a master's degree?
*6. What is a Ph.D.?

3. Teachers

Dialog

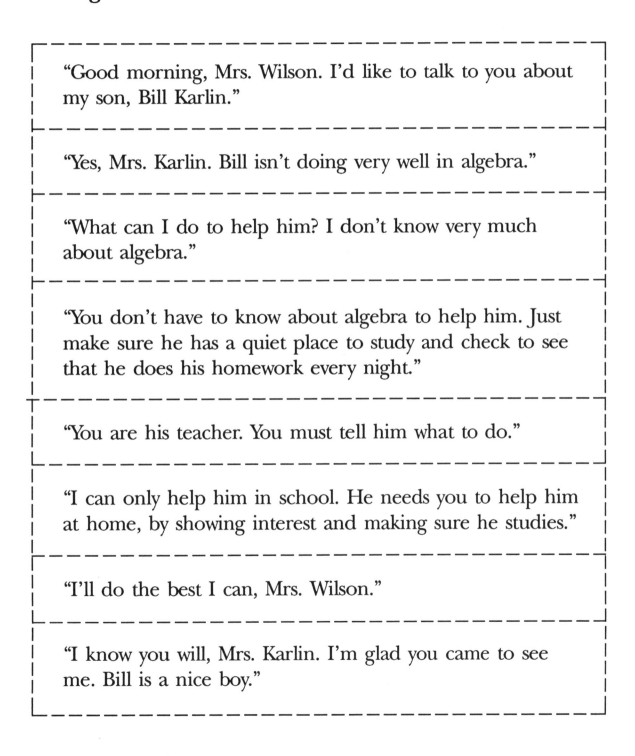

"Good morning, Mrs. Wilson. I'd like to talk to you about my son, Bill Karlin."

"Yes, Mrs. Karlin. Bill isn't doing very well in algebra."

"What can I do to help him? I don't know very much about algebra."

"You don't have to know about algebra to help him. Just make sure he has a quiet place to study and check to see that he does his homework every night."

"You are his teacher. You must tell him what to do."

"I can only help him in school. He needs you to help him at home, by showing interest and making sure he studies."

"I'll do the best I can, Mrs. Wilson."

"I know you will, Mrs. Karlin. I'm glad you came to see me. Bill is a nice boy."

Questions for Understanding

Ask the students these questions.

1. Who came to see Mrs. Wilson?
2. How is Bill doing at school?
3. What does Mrs. Wilson want Bill to do every night?
4. What can Mrs. Karlin do to help Bill?

Questions for Discussion and Composition

Present these questions as a basis for class discussions or writing assignments.

1. What university degrees can a person earn in the United States?
2. What university degrees can a person earn in your native country?
3. In what ways should parents be involved in their children's education?

Activities

Assign these activities to individuals, small groups, or the whole class to reinforce and expand on the lesson topic.

1. Make a list of the qualities a good teacher should have. Rank them in order of importance. Then compare your list to your classmates' lists.
2. Conduct a survey of the teachers in your school to find out how many have bachelor's degrees, master's degrees, and doctorates. Make a chart or graph to show the results of your survey.
3. Choose a profession that interests you. Make a list of the university degrees, skills, or special training a person must have to be qualified for this profession.

4. Car Troubles

Narrative

My car wouldn't start last Tuesday.

I had to call a tow truck to take it to a garage.

The head mechanic looked at my car, and then he gave me a big smile. I knew I was in trouble.

The engine needed work, and so did the transmission.

He said it would take three days to fix my car.

I had to take the bus to work.

After three days I called the garage.

My car wasn't finished because the head mechanic was sick.

The other mechanics weren't sure when the car would be fixed.

They only knew it needed a lot of work.

The mechanics told me to call back again in a week.

I don't want to be a moaner, but couldn't they give me a loaner?

Questions for Understanding

Ask the students these questions. (The answer to the starred question is not provided in the narrative.)

1. What happened to the car?
2. How did the car get to the garage?
3. What happened to the head mechanic?
4. When will the car be ready?
*5. What is a **loaner**?

4. Car Troubles

Dialog

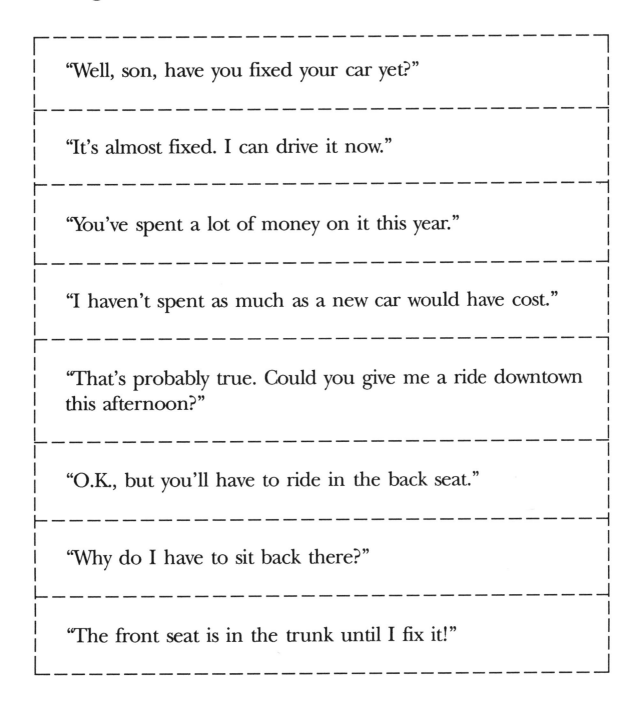

"Well, son, have you fixed your car yet?"

"It's almost fixed. I can drive it now."

"You've spent a lot of money on it this year."

"I haven't spent as much as a new car would have cost."

"That's probably true. Could you give me a ride downtown this afternoon?"

"O.K., but you'll have to ride in the back seat."

"Why do I have to sit back there?"

"The front seat is in the trunk until I fix it!"

Questions for Understanding

Ask the students these questions.

1. Who is talking in this dialog?
2. Why is the father concerned about his son's car?
3. What favor does the father ask his son?
4. What part of the car still needs to be fixed?

Questions for Discussion and Composition

Present these questions as a basis for class discussions or writing assignments.

1. What experience(s) have you had with auto repairs?
2. What are the advantages and disadvantages of owning a car?
3. How can owning a car change your life?
4. Why do some people distrust auto mechanics?

Activities

Assign these activities to individuals, small groups, or the whole class to reinforce and expand on the lesson topic.

1. Write a newspaper advertisement to sell a car.
2. Collect pictures and make a collage that shows how cars have changed from 1900 to the present.
3. Conduct a survey to compare prices for the following car repairs:
   a. changing the oil and oil filter
   b. changing the air filter
   c. fixing a flat tire
   d. overhauling a carburetor
   e. replacing a battery

   Make a chart showing the average cost of making each repair at a local gas station, at a car dealership, and at home. (Be sure to include the cost of parts and labor.)

5. City Transportation

Narrative

It is difficult to get around in some big cities if you don't know the bus system.

First, you have to learn how the streets are laid out, so you can choose the best route to get where you want to go.

Then you have to figure out which buses to take.

When you know how many buses you need to take, you can figure out the fare.

You can usually buy a transfer if you need to take more than one bus.

Most bus drivers are helpful. If you ask them, they will tell you where to get off and where to wait for the next bus.

All the buses along one route have the same number. You can tell which bus to get on by its number.

After you have ridden the buses for a while, you will begin to know them as well as you know your name.

Questions for Understanding

Ask the students these questions.

1. What do you need to know before you can figure out which bus to take?
2. What is a **transfer**?
3. How can a bus driver help you?
4. When you see a bus, how can you tell if it's the one you want to take?

5. City Transportation

Dialog

"Does the 23 bus stop here?"

"No, it doesn't. Where do you want to go?"

"I'm trying to get to the train station. I have to be there by noon!"

"Well, the 23 bus won't help you. You need the 143."

"Where can I catch that bus? It's getting late!"

"Take this bus, and then transfer to the 143 at Broadway Street."

"Which way should I go on Broadway?"

"You need to go east. I'll show you when we get there."

"I don't know if I have enough change for two buses."

"Don't worry. I'll sell you a transfer for the 143."

"Thanks for all your help."

"No problem. Just hurry; other people are waiting to get on."

Questions for Understanding

Ask the students these questions.

1. Where does the passenger want to go?
2. What bus does he or she need to take?
3. How did the bus driver help the passenger?
4. How could the passenger afford to take two buses?

Questions for Discussion and Composition

Present these questions as a basis for class discussions or writing assignments.

1. What good and bad experiences have you had riding buses?
2. How does a bus ride in the United States compare with a bus ride in your native country?
3. Compare the advantages and disadvantages of driving your own car and riding the bus.

Activities

Assign these activities to individuals, small groups, or the whole class to reinforce and expand on the lesson topic.

1. Use local maps and bus schedules to show how and when your class could travel from school to various places in your community.
2. Design an advertisement for your school that could be placed on the outside of a bus.
3. Write a letter to your community's bus service praising something you like about the service.
4. Conduct a survey to see how many of the students in your class ride the local buses regularly. Make a chart or graph to show the results of your survey.

6. A Birthday Party

Narrative

On her fifth birthday, my sister Lois had a party with seven friends.

Our parents cleaned and decorated the house and prepared refreshments before the party.

The first guest arrived with a large gift.

Twins arrived next with one small gift.

Lois didn't want to let one of them come in.

After all the guests arrived, the children played some games.

Then Lois opened her gifts.

Next they all played on the swings in the backyard.

When it was time for cake, they ran into the house.

The children all sang "Happy Birthday," and Lois blew out the candles.

Then the children got wild. Some of them even put cake in their milk and ice cream in their hair!

It's a good thing birthdays only come once a year.

Questions for Understanding

1. Why did Lois's parents clean the house?
2. What happened when the twins brought one gift?
3. What did the children do at the party?
4. What refreshments were served at the party?

6. A Birthday Party

Dialog

"What's wrong, honey?"

"Lois is having a birthday party on Saturday and she didn't invite me."

"How do you know?"

"I heard some kids talking about it at school today."

"I thought you and Lois were friends."

"We were, but we aren't anymore."

"What happened? Did you have a fight about something?"

"No. She just doesn't like me anymore."

"Oh, I'm sure she still likes you. Maybe she didn't think you'd want to come to her party."

"Well, I wouldn't! Who cares about her dumb old party anyway?"

"I can see you don't. Well, maybe we can do something special by ourselves on Saturday."

"Great! Let's go to the zoo!"

Questions for Understanding

Ask the students these questions.

1. Who is talking in this dialog?
2. Who is having a party?
3. Why is this child unhappy?
4. How does the parent try to help the child?
5. Do you think the parent handled this situation well? Why or why not?

Questions for Discussion and Composition

Present these questions as a basis for class discussions and writing assignments.

1. Compare and contrast traditions for celebrating birthdays in various cultures.
2. What kinds of birthday gifts would be appropriate for the following people?

    a young child

    a friend

    a grandparent

    a teacher

    a parent

3. What would you do if your child wasn't invited to a classmate's party?
4. What can be done to avoid hurting people's feelings when inviting guests to a party?

Activities

Assign these activities to individuals, small groups, or the whole class to reinforce and expand on the lesson topic.

1. Make a chart or graph showing when the students in your class have their birthdays.
2. Plan a birthday party for a ten-year-old. Choose appropriate food, decorations, and activities.
3. Design a birthday card for each of the following people.

    a teacher

    a friend

    a parent

    a sister

    a brother

    a grandparent

7. Before the Soccer Match

Narrative

Today I learned how important it is to be neat.

I had planned to play soccer with my friends in a neighborhood match at the park.

Just as I was ready to leave, my mother demanded that I clean my room.

I told her I had already cleaned it and organized all my things.

She looked into my room and said, "I can't believe you think this mess is neat."

The room looked good to me.

"This place looks like a pigpen! How can a son of mine live like this?"

She really made me feel bad. So I started cleaning again.

I threw out some stuff I had saved for years. I even got rid of the stuffed frog I won at the school carnival last year.

While I was cleaning, I found a homework paper that was due last week.

My room was clean, but I was in trouble with my friends. Our team lost the game.

Only four members of our team showed up. I guess the other players had to stay home and clean their bedrooms, too!

Questions for Understanding

Ask the students these questions.

1. Why didn't this person go to the soccer game?
2. What did he have to do? Why?
3. Name some things he found in his room.
4. Why did his team lose the game?

7. Before the Soccer Match

Dialog

"I don't think there will be a soccer game today. It's really raining hard."

"That's no problem! We're not afraid of a little rain."

"But it's cold and windy, too. The field will be all muddy."

"That's no problem! We can play on a muddy field."

"You'll get your uniform all dirty if you play on that field."

"That's no problem! My uniform can be washed."

"I'm your mother, and you're only eight years old. I say you can't play soccer today."

"That's a big problem!"

Questions for Understanding

Ask the students these questions.

1. Why doesn't the mother want her child to play soccer today?
2. Why does the child think it would be all right to play?
3. What kind of day is it?
4. Do you agree with the mother's decision not to let her child play soccer? Why or why not?

Questions for Discussion and Composition

Present these questions as a basis for class discussions or writing assignments.

1. How are sports events different when they're played in the rain?
2. What experiences have you had that were significant because they happened in the rain?
3. How does the weather affect people?
4. What do you like to do on cold and rainy days?

Activities

Assign these activities to individuals, small groups, or the whole class to reinforce and expand on the lesson topic.

1. Make bulletin boards that illustrate sports from various countries. Show and label the uniforms, equipment, and some of the activities of each sport.
2. Collect photographs of some famous athletes. Label each one with the person's name, native country, and sport.
3. Choose a local sports team to support as a class. Follow the team's progress through the season by reading newspaper reports. Try to attend some of the games, too.
4. Have the class or individual students choose a sports team or an athlete to write letters to.

8. Social Life

Narrative

You'll never guess what happened to me last week. Let me tell you.

I finally found a dress I liked for the dance.

I found not only one but two dresses that looked good on me, a blue one and a peach one.

I chose the blue dress. Then I went to a shoe store to get shoes dyed to match it.

The next day after school I went to Pamela Sue's house. You won't believe what happened.

She showed me **her** new dress for the dance.

It was the same dress I had chosen! I was in a panic.

I hurried back to the store and returned the dress.

Then I bought the peach dress.

Next I went back to the shoe store. They told me my shoes were already dyed blue.

They said the only color they could make them now was black.

Can you imagine black shoes at a spring dance?

Questions for Understanding

Ask the students these questions.

1. Where is this person going?
2. How many dresses did she find?
3. What did Pamela Sue already have?
4. Why was this a problem?
5. What was the problem with the shoes?
6. Was this a very important problem?

8. Social Life

Dialog

"Did we get any mail today?"

"We got an invitation to a surprise party for Uncle Joe."

"Oh! I hate surprise parties. They always make people tell lies."

"I think they're a lot of fun."

"Fun? You usually have to sneak into someone's house and wait until they get home."

"Yes, but while you wait you can decorate and fix the refreshments."

"I still don't understand why you'd want to do that to a friend."

"We throw surprise parties to show friends that we like them enough to do something nice for them."

"Nice! When the person arrives, everybody jumps up and yells 'Surprise!' You really think that's a nice thing to do?"

"Sure! The person always smiles and looks happy."

"Most people look like they're going to have a heart attack. I'd hate it if anyone gave me a surprise party."

"Well, I guess we'll have to cancel this party then. It isn't really for Uncle Joe; it's for you."

Questions for Understanding

Ask the students these questions.

1. Who is talking in this dialog?
2. What is a surprise party?
3. How do you plan a surprise party?
4. Why does one of these speakers dislike surprise parties?
5. Who was supposed to be surprised at this party?

Questions for Discussion and Composition

Present these questions as a basis for class discussions or writing assignments.

1. What are appropriate clothes to wear to each of these activities?

   a wedding

   a beach party

   a baseball game

   an evening at a play

   a school dance

   a birthday party at a fancy restaurant

   a black-tie dinner

   a dinner at your boss's home

   a job interview

2. What kinds of social activities do you enjoy? What kinds of social activities do you dislike? Give reasons for your answers.

3. What is your "friendship style"? Do you prefer to spend time with a few close friends, with many acquaintances, or by yourself? Why?

Activities

Assign these activities to individuals, small groups, or the whole class to reinforce and expand on the lesson topic.

1. Design an invitation to a party, dance, wedding, or other social event.
2. Write a letter to a friend or relative describing a social event you have attended recently.
3. Arrange magazine pictures to tell a story about modern fashions.

9. Buying Music

Narrative

I like rock-and-roll music, but I hardly ever get to listen to it.

In the morning, everyone else in my family wants to listen to the news on the radio.

When I get to work, there is classical music playing in the lobby.

Then I go up to my office. The music in the elevator is really terrible.

Music is piped into my office, but my company only allows "easy-listening" music.

After work, I like to stop at a music store.

Then I can buy the kind of music I like to listen to at home.

That's when I have trouble with my family.

I turn on my new music to listen to it the way I like it.

Someone always shouts "Turn it down!"

I have to wear earphones to listen to my own music.

At least I don't have to listen to elevator music at home!

Questions for Understanding

Ask the students these questions.

1. What kind of music does this person like?
2. Why does this person have trouble listening to his or her favorite kind of music?
3. Does anyone else mentioned in the narrative like rock music?
4. What kind of music does this person like the least?

9. Buying Music

Dialog

"Excuse me. Do you have the latest album by the Bright Shouts?"

"Which one do you want? The original or the re-mix?"

"I don't know. It's not for me. It's for my friend's birthday."

"Well, a lot of people don't like the re-mix."

"Can I listen to both of them before I decide?"

"I'm sorry, but there's no way we can do that."

"I don't know what to do now. Which version do they play on the radio?"

"I hear the original a lot, but don't go by me. I don't like the Bright Shouts."

"What groups do you like? Maybe I'll get something different for my friend."

"To tell you the truth, my favorite group is the Bach String Quartet."

"I've never heard of them. What do they sing?"

"They don't sing. They're a classical string quartet that plays a lot of Bach. I don't like rock and roll."

Questions for Understanding

Ask the students these questions.

1. Why is this person shopping for music?
2. Does the shopper know what he or she wants to buy?
3. Can shoppers listen to music in the store before buying it?
4. What kind of music does the salesperson like?

Questions for Discussion and Composition

Present these questions as a basis for class discussions or writing assignments.

1. What kind(s) of concerts do you enjoy? What do you like about them?
2. In what ways is a rock concert different from a symphony concert?
3. How does music influence the way people behave and feel?
4. In your opinion, should music with violent or explicitly sexual lyrics be censored or labeled? Why or why not?

Activities

Assign these activities to individuals, small groups, or the whole class to reinforce and expand on the lesson topic.

1. Write lyrics for a song about an issue that concerns you.
2. Write a fan letter to a performing artist or group.
3. Give an oral presentation comparing and contrasting two different styles of music.
4. Write a short essay about the history and development of your favorite type of music.

10. Holiday Shopping

Narrative

Yesterday I went shopping for holiday gifts for my family. It took me all day just to buy a gift for my mother!

When I got to the store in the morning, it was already crowded with other shoppers.

I spent a long time looking for the size I needed, because there weren't any salespeople to help me.

Then I had to wait in a long line to pay for my gift.

The girl at the cash register told me I had to go to customer service to get a box.

At the customer service counter there were two long lines.

The longest line was just to get a box.

The other line was for fancy gift wrap.

Fancy gift wrap costs two dollars, but I took the shortest line because I was in a hurry.

When I got to the front of the line, the clerk took my gift and told me it would be ready in an hour.

I went to get something to eat. When I came back, I had to stand in line again to get my wrapped gift.

Now I'm worried because I have ten more gifts to buy, and there are only seven days left until the holiday!

Questions for Understanding

Ask the students these questions.

1. Why did it take so long to shop for one gift?
2. Do you think this shopper is a man or a woman? Why?
3. Why was the line for fancy gift wrap shorter?
4. Was it really faster for this shopper to choose fancy gift wrap?
5. Do you think this shopper will finish his or her shopping before the holiday?

10. Holiday Shopping

Dialog

"How was your shopping trip with the kids?"

"Exhausting! Tim didn't want to look for a gift for his teacher. He only wanted to look at the toys in the toy store."

"Did he ever decide on a gift?"

"He finally chose a box of candy."

"His teacher will like that. Did Tina find gifts for her friends?"

"She got them all stationery, but she wasn't happy about it."

"What did she want to buy?"

"She looked at a lot of things, but they all cost over twenty dollars."

"That was too much to spend, since she had seven friends to buy gifts for."

"That's what I thought! I didn't want to spend a hundred and fifty dollars on a bunch of teenage girls."

"Did you buy anything else?"

"No. I wanted to buy you a gift, but the kids wore me out and spent all my money!"

Questions for Understanding

Ask the students these questions.

1. Who is talking in this dialog?
2. Who went shopping?
3. What did they need to buy?
4. What kinds of gifts did the daughter want to buy?
5. Do you think the children chose nice gifts?
6. What else did the shopper want to buy? Why didn't he or she buy it?

Questions for Discussion and Composition

Present these questions as a basis for class discussions or writing assignments.

1. On which holidays do Americans normally give gifts?
2. On which holidays do people in your native country normally give gifts?
3. For whom do you buy holiday gifts?
4. What kinds of holiday gifts might be appropriate for these people?

> an elementary school teacher
>
> a junior high school teacher
>
> a high school teacher
>
> a boss
>
> a classmate of the same sex
>
> a classmate of the opposite sex

5. What is the most unusual holiday gift you have ever received?
6. Do you think children should receive toys or clothes as holiday gifts?

Activities

Assign these activities to individuals, small groups, or the whole class to reinforce and expand on the lesson topic.

1. Design gift wrapping paper for these holidays:

Christmas	birthday
Chanukah	graduation
Valentine's Day	birth of a baby
Mother's Day	wedding
Father's Day	anniversary

2. Prepare and present a radio commercial for a department store advertising that people will receive quick service during their holiday shopping.
3. Make a list of economical and/or ecological gifts you could give as an alternative to traditional holiday gifts.

Part

2

Interviews and and Match-Ups

Ownership

Find people who have these things. Have them sign your paper.

1. a red shirt _____

2. black shoes _____

3. a white T-shirt _____

4. blue pants _____

5. a yellow dress _____

6. plaid shorts _____

7. a tie _____

8. a jacket _____

9. a hat _____

10. glasses _____

11. a skirt _____

12. a belt _____

13. blue socks _____

14. a handkerchief _____

15. a yellow blouse _____

16. white tennis shoes _____

17. a white purse _____

18. gold jewelry _____

19. a wristwatch _____

20. silver earrings _____

21. a silver belt buckle _____

22. jeans _____

23. boots _____

24. a sports coat _____

25. high heels _____

Everyday Actions

Find people who do and don't do these things. Have them sign your paper.

1. work on Saturdays   _____

2. wash the dishes at home   _____

3. play chess   _____

4. drive a car   _____

5. wear one earring   _____

6. play the guitar   _____

7. sing in a choir   _____

8. don't work after school   _____

9. don't eat lunch at school   _____

10. don't wear jeans   _____

11. don't bring paper to school   _____

12. don't eat ice cream   _____

13. go to the library   _____

14. listen to music on the radio in the morning   _____

15. read a newspaper every day   _____

16. feed a pet   _____

17. buy food in a supermarket   _____

18. whistle   _____

19. ride a bicycle to school   _____

20. do homework every night   _____

21. walk to school   _____

22. don't type   _____

23. don't eat fish   _____

24. don't run in the morning   _____

25. don't baby-sit   _____

Things People Can and Can't Do

Find people who can and can't do these things. Have them sign your paper.

1. can whistle _____

2. can bake a cherry pie _____

3. can ride a bicycle _____

4. can sew on a machine _____

5. can change a tire _____

6. can't whistle _____

7. can't drive a car _____

8. can't play the piano _____

9. can't go to the movies on Saturday nights _____

10. can't eat eggs _____

11. can sing very well _____

12. can play a musical instrument _____

13. can keep a pet at home _____

14. can swim _____

15. can speak three languages _____

16. can ice-skate _____

17. can't read in a moving car _____

18. can't speak Spanish _____

19. can't type _____

20. can't stay out until midnight on a school night _____

21. can milk a cow _____

22. can juggle _____

23. can do a headstand _____

24. can knit _____

25. can play tennis _____

Things People Did and Didn't Do

Find people who did and did not do these things. Have them sign your paper.

1. ate breakfast this morning   _____

2. played basketball last Saturday   _____

3. visited relatives last weekend   _____

4. talked on the telephone after 7:00 last night   _____

5. watched TV after 11:30 last night   _____

6. did not eat dinner at home last night   _____

7. did not watch TV last night   _____

8. did not read a book last week   _____

9. did not go to the beach last summer   _____

10. did not do homework last night   _____

11. changed a baby's diaper last week   _____

12. broke a school rule last week   _____

13. kissed someone yesterday   _____

14. wore a coat to school today   _____

15. gave someone a birthday card last week   _____

16. did not read a magazine last week   _____

17. did not move here from another country   _____

18. did not bring any money to school today   _____

19. did not bring a lunch to school today   _____

20. did not stay at home last Saturday night   _____

21. did not grow up on a farm   _____

22. did not sleep well last night   _____

23. walked to school today   _____

24. read the newspaper this morning   _____

25. wrote a letter last week   _____

Things People Will and Won't Do

Find people who will or won't do these things. Have them sign your paper.

1. will read a book today   _____

2. will eat in the cafeteria tomorrow   _____

3. will listen to the news in English tonight   _____

4. will buy new clothes this week   _____

5. won't watch TV tonight   _____

6. won't go to a bank today   _____

7. won't talk on the telephone today   _____

8. won't eat ice cream tonight   _____

9. will go fishing this month   _____

10. will spend a night in a hotel this week   _____

11. will visit a sick friend in the next two days   _____

12. will get a paycheck on Friday   _____

13. will work and study before tomorrow   _____

14. will go grocery shopping today   _____

15. won't drink fruit juice this week   _____

16. won't work on Saturday   _____

17. won't do laundry tomorrow   _____

18. will go to the dentist next week   _____

19. will feed a pet before tomorrow   _____

20. will drive a car tonight   _____

21. will write a letter tonight   _____

22. won't bring food to school tomorrow   _____

23. won't cook dinner tonight   _____

24. will go to a rock concert this month   _____

25. will exercise tomorrow morning   _____

Things People Have Done

Find people who have done these things. Have them sign your paper.

1. have seen a frog   _____

2. have flown in an airplane   _____

3. have eaten snails   _____

4. have driven a car   _____

5. have taken an animal to school   _____

6. have been to the zoo   _____

7. have found a wallet in the street _____

8. have been to a wedding   _____

9. have slept on the ground   _____

10. have spoken to a police officer   _____

11. have traveled by train   _____

12. have flown a kite   _____

13. have heard an elephant trumpet _____

14. have written a letter to a government official _____

15. have broken a dish   _____

Things People Haven't Done

Find people who have **not** done these things. Have them sign your paper.

1. haven't worked on a farm   _____

2. haven't cleaned the inside of an oven   _____

3. haven't played a musical instrument   _____

4. haven't walked on a beach   _____

5. haven't hiked in the mountains   _____

6. haven't waited for a bus   _____

7. haven't painted a picture   _____

8. haven't washed a car   _____

9. haven't used a typewriter   _____

10. haven't fixed a bicycle   _____

11. haven't changed a baby's diaper   _____

12. haven't caught a fish   _____

13. haven't talked to the school principal   _____

14. haven't played in the snow   _____

15. haven't worried about a test   _____

Things Pairs of People Have and Haven't Done

Find two people who have or haven't done each of these things. Have them sign your paper.

1. They have seen an animal bigger than a cow.

   _____   _____

2. They have fixed a flat tire on a car.

   _____   _____

3. They have cooked dinner and washed the dishes by themselves.

   _____   _____

4. They have planted flowers in a garden or a pot.

   _____   _____

5. They have worked in a factory.

   _____   _____

6. They have called somebody in another country on the telephone.

   _____   _____

7. They have never pushed a car to a gas station.

   _____   _____

8. They have never driven all night in a car.

   _____   _____

9. They have never slept in a hotel.

   _____   _____

10. They have never shouted at a bus driver.

    _____   _____

11. They have never climbed a tree.

    _____   _____

12. They have never taken a nap in a park.

    _____   _____

Things People Will Have Done

Find people who will have done these things. Have them sign your paper.

1. will have held a baby before tomorrow   _____

2. will have eaten fish before tomorrow   _____

3. will have read a newspaper before class tomorrow   _____

4. will have seen a movie before Monday   _____

5. will have written a letter by noon tomorrow   _____

6. will have cooked before going to bed tonight   _____

7. will have been to a party before next Monday   _____

8. will have bought new clothes by next week   _____

9. will have received a paycheck by Saturday   _____

10. will have broken a promise by midnight   _____

11. will have petted a dog before class tomorrow   _____

12. will have gone on a trip by the end of the year   _____

13. will have baked cookies by the end of the week   _____

14. will have received a gift before next week   _____

15. will have sung a song before bedtime   _____

Movie Survey

Ask twenty-five people these questions. Count how many people answer "yes" and how many answer "no."

1. Have you gone to a movie in the last month?

   Yes _____

   No _____

2. Do you usually buy food at a movie theater?

   Yes _____

   No _____

3. Do you think most movie theaters are kept clean?

   Yes _____

   No _____

4. Do you think movies cost too much money?

   Yes _____

   No _____

Now use the information you gathered to finish these sentences.

1. _____ % of these people went to a movie in the last month.

2. _____ % of these people think movies cost too much money.

3. _____ % of these people think most movie theaters are dirty.

4. _____ % of these people usually buy food to eat in movie theaters.

5. I think these results tell us that _____

_____

_____.

What Am I?

Before class, copy and cut apart the animal name cards. Then, as the students enter the room, tape one card to each student's back without showing him or her what it says. On a signal, have the students move around the room asking each other questions about the animals. The object is for each student to guess which animal name is on his or her back. The students may ask any question except "What kind of animal am I?" Some good questions include "Where do I live?" "What do I eat?" and "What color am I?" Students may ask only one question of each classmate and must answer one question from each classmate. When they think they know what animal they are, they may ask a classmate "Am I a _____?" You may wish to have the students sit down once they have correctly identified the names of their animals; however, these students should continue to participate by answering questions asked by their classmates. The activity ends when all the students have correctly identified what they are.

bear	grasshopper	shark
bee	horse	sheep
buffalo	kangaroo	skunk
chicken	leopard	snake
cow	lion	spider
deer	monkey	squirrel
elephant	mouse	tiger
fox	parrot	turkey
frog	pig	turtle
giraffe	porcupine	whale
goat	rabbit	wolf
gorilla	rat	zebra

What Am I? Crossword Puzzle

Complete this puzzle using the clues below.

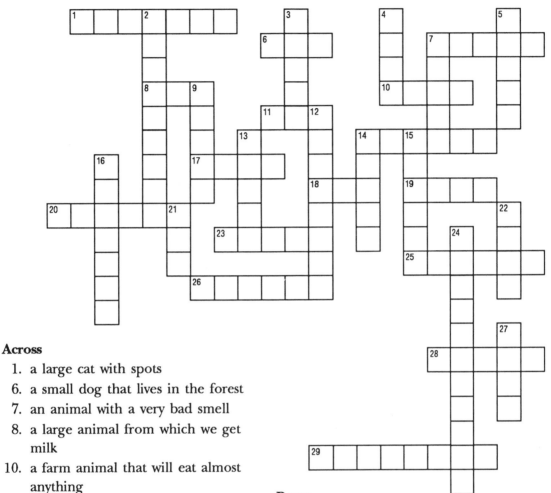

Across

1. a large cat with spots
6. a small dog that lives in the forest
7. an animal with a very bad smell
8. a large animal from which we get milk
10. a farm animal that will eat almost anything
11. an insect that makes honey
14. a large bird we eat at Thanksgiving
17. a big cat that lives in Africa
18. the animal from which we get bacon and ham
19. a big, dangerous animal that lives in the forest
20. a small animal that has eight legs
23. an animal that looks like a horse with stripes
25. an animal that moves very slowly
26. a bird that can say words
28. an animal that gives us wool
29. an animal that lives in a tree and eats nuts

Down

2. an animal that has very sharp spines
3. Mickey _____
4. a green animal that hops
5. an animal that moves without feet
7. a large, dangerous fish
9. a huge animal that lives in the water
12. a large animal with a trunk
13. an animal we can ride
14. a large, striped cat
15. Bugs Bunny is a _____
16. a bird whose eggs we eat
21. an animal that looks like a big mouse
22. a dangerous dog that lives in the mountains
24. an insect that can jump far
27. a hoofed animal that can run fast

Participle Match-Up

Before class, copy and cut apart the verb cards. Then, during class, give each student a card. On a signal, have the students move around the room trying to match the base forms of the verbs with their past participles. The students should not show their cards to each other until they think they have found their correct partners. As the partners find each other, they should move to the front of the room and stand in pairs. When all the students have come to the front of the room, let the pairs read their cards and give the class an opportunity to approve or disapprove the matches. If any pairs are matched incorrectly, the class should work together to correct the matches.

be	been
break	broken
bring	brought
build	built
dig	dug
eat	eaten
fall	fallen
fight	fought
fly	flown
freeze	frozen
go	gone

(continued on next page)

grow	grown
hear	heard
hide	hidden
keep	kept
light	lit
pay	paid
read	read
sleep	slept
take	taken
tell	told

Participle Crossword Puzzle

Complete this puzzle using the past participles of the verbs listed below.

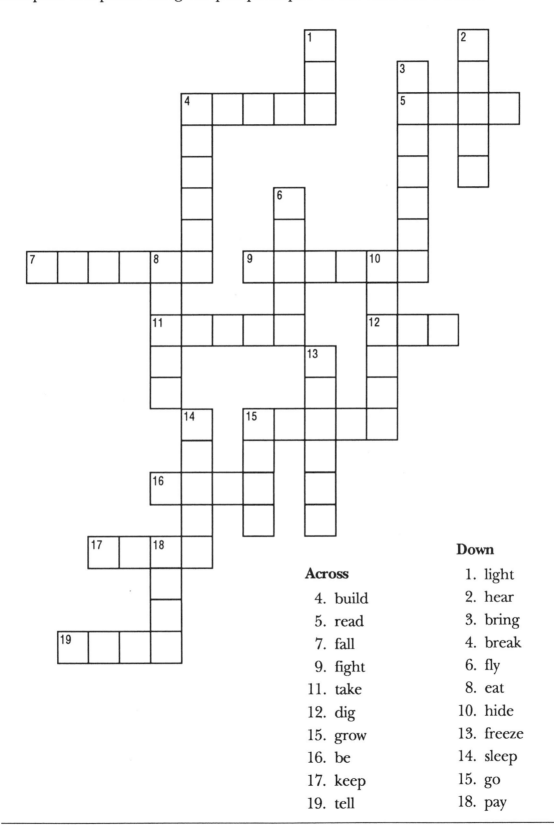

Across

4. build
5. read
7. fall
9. fight
11. take
12. dig
15. grow
16. be
17. keep
19. tell

Down

1. light
2. hear
3. bring
4. break
6. fly
8. eat
10. hide
13. freeze
14. sleep
15. go
18. pay

Around the House Match-Up

Before class, copy and cut apart the word and definition cards. Then, during class, give each student a card. On a signal, have the students move around the room trying to match the words with the correct definitions. The students should not show their cards to each other until they think they have found their correct partners. As the partners find each other, they should move to the front of the room and stand in pairs. When all the students have come to the front of the room, let the pairs read their cards and give the class an opportunity to approve or disapprove the matches. If any pairs are matched incorrectly, the class should work together to correct the matches.

to bathe	to wash one's body in a tub of water
bedroom	a room for sleeping
bookcase	a place to keep books
to clean	to remove dirt or dust
to cook	to heat food and prepare it for eating
door	the entrance to a building or a room
to drive	to operate a vehicle such as a car
food	things to eat
garden	a piece of land where flowers, fruit, or vegetables are grown

(continued on next page)

glass	a hard material you can see through
knife	a tool for cutting
lawn mower	a machine that cuts grass
to mail	to send letters or packages through the post office
newspaper	a printed paper containing the news of the day
pet	an animal that is kept at home
photograph	a picture taken with a camera
refrigerator	a machine that keeps food cold and fresh
sandwich	two pieces of bread with meat or some other food between them
to sleep	to rest with your eyes closed and not knowing what is happening
vacuum cleaner	a machine that sucks up dirt

Around the House Crossword Puzzle

Complete this puzzles using the clues below.

Across

1. a hard material you can see through
3. two pieces of bread with meat or some other food between them
4. a _____ cleaner is used to suck up dirt
8. washing one's body in a tub of water
9. to operate a vehicle such as a car
11. things to eat
12. to heat food and prepare it for eating
14. a place to keep books
15. a printed paper containing the news of the day
17. a tool for cutting

Down

2. a machine that cuts grass
5. an animal that is kept at home
6. to send letters or packages through the post office
7. a machine that keeps food cold and fresh
8. a room for sleeping
9. the entrance to a building or a room
10. a picture taken with a camera
12. to remove dirt or dust
13. a piece of land where flowers, fruit, or vegetables are grown
16. to rest with your eyes closed and not knowing what is happening

Occupation Match-Up

Before class, copy and cut apart the occupation and description cards. Then, during class, give each student a card. On a signal, have the students move around the room trying to match the names of the occupations with their descriptions. The students should not show their cards to each other until they think they have found their correct partners. As the partners find each other, they should move to the front of the room and stand in pairs. When all the students have come to the front of the room, let the pairs read their cards and give the class an opportunity to approve or disapprove the matches. If any pairs are matched incorrectly, the class should work together to correct the matches.

accountant	I keep records of money paid and received.
architect	I design buildings.
athlete	I am trained or skilled at sports.
carpenter	I make things out of wood.
cashier	I receive money in a restaurant or store.
chef	I prepare food in a restaurant.
doctor	I help sick people get well.
executive	I control or direct a business.
gardener	I grow and care for plants.
lawyer	I help people with legal matters.
mechanic	I repair machines such as cars and trucks.

(continued on next page)

musician	I play an instrument, sing, or write music.
painter	I paint walls and other surfaces.
pharmacist	I prepare medicines ordered by a doctor.
photographer	I take pictures with a camera.
plumber	I connect and repair sinks, toilets, and water and sewer pipes.
police officer	I enforce the laws.
programmer	I give coded instructions to computers.
psychologist	I study behavior and help people with emotional problems.
receptionist	I greet people when they enter an office.
repair person	I fix broken things such as appliances.
salesperson	I sell things in a store.
secretary	I help with correspondence and other business matters in an office.
tailor	I make or change the fit of clothing.
teacher	I help people learn things.

Occupation Crossword Puzzle

Complete this puzzle using the clues below.

Across

3. gives coded instructions to computers
8. repairs machines such as cars and trucks
9. helps people learn things
10. makes or changes the fit of clothing
12. controls or directs a business
14. prepares medicines ordered by a doctor
16. is trained or skilled at sports
17. a chef prepares food in a _____
18. studies behavior and helps people with emotional problems
19. helps people with legal matters
20. sells things in a store

Down

1. connects and repairs sinks, toilets, and water and sewer pipes
2. helps sick people get well
3. paints walls and other surfaces
4. grows and cares for plants
5. keeps records of money paid and received
6. a _____ person fixes broken things such as appliances
7. receives money in a restaurant or store
11. helps with correspondence and other business matters in an office
13. makes things out of wood
15. plays an instrument, sings, or writes music

Greeting Card Match-Up

Many ESL students have trouble buying appropriate greeting cards. This exercise helps students match phrases commonly used in greeting cards with the appropriate occasions for sending the cards.

Before class, copy and cut apart the cards. Then, during class, give each student a card. On a signal, have the students move around the room trying to match the greeting card phrases with the appropriate occasions. The students should not show their cards to each other until they think they have found their correct partners. As the partners find each other, they should move to the front of the room and stand in pairs. When all the students have come to the front of the room, let the pairs read their cards and give the class an opportunity to approve or disapprove the matches. If any pairs are matched incorrectly, the class should work together to correct the matches.

As You Tie the Knot	to express your best wishes for a man and woman as they get married
A Bar Mitzvah Wish for You	to express best wishes to a Jewish boy at a celebration of his thirteenth birthday
Belated Birthday Wishes	to wish someone a happy birthday after the actual date
Bon Voyage	to wish someone a good trip
Congratulations	to tell someone you are happy that something good happened to him or her
For Your Baby Shower	to express best wishes to a woman or a couple at a party before their baby is born
For Your Bridal Shower	to express best wishes to a woman at a party before her wedding
For Your Silver Wedding Anniversary	to recognize that a couple has been married for 25 years

(continued on next page)

Happy Anniversary to the One I Love	to celebrate with your husband or wife on the date you were married
Happy Holidays	to express best wishes during the winter season near Christmas, New Year's and Chanukah
I'm Here for You	to tell someone that you are willing to help him or her
In Appreciation for Your Thoughtfulness	to say thank you to someone who has done something nice
Keep in Touch	to tell someone who lives far away that you want to remain friends and exchange letters and/or phone calls
Missing You	to tell someone who is far away that you wish you could see him or her
On Your Engagement	to express wishes to someone who has made plans to get married
Thinking of You	to tell someone that you care and are concerned about him or her
We Can Work It Out	to tell a friend with whom you had a disagreement that you want to be friends again
Welcome Back	to tell someone you are happy they have returned from a trip or a hospital stay
Wishing You a Quick Recovery	to tell someone you hope he or she will feel well soon
With Sympathy in Your Time of Sorrow	to tell someone you are sorry that his or her relative or close friend has died
With Warmest Thanks	to tell someone you appreciate a gift or a kind action

Greeting Card Crossword Puzzle

Complete this puzzle using the clues below.

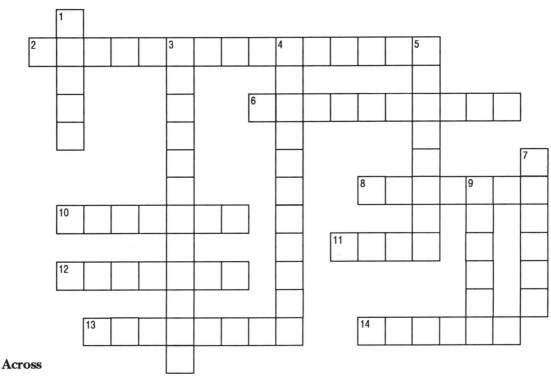

Across

2. When you want to tell someone you are happy that something good happened to him or her, you say "_____."

6. When two people make plans to get married, you may send a card that says "On Your _____."

8. When a Jewish boy turns thirteen, he may celebrate with a Bar _____ ceremony.

10. When someone you care about is far away, you might send a card that says "_____ You."

11. A party given for a pregnant woman is a _____ shower.

12. When you miss someone's birthday, you can send a card that says "_____ Birthday Wishes."

13. When someone you know is ill or injured, you might send a card that says "Wishing You a Quick _____."

14. A party given for an engaged woman is a bridal _____.

Down

1. When you don't want to lose contact with someone, you say "Keep in _____."

3. Sending a thank-you card shows your _____ for something nice someone has done.

4. The date a man and woman were married is their _____.

5. A _____ card shows your sorrow at someone's death.

7. To show appreciation for something, you could send a card that says "With Warmest _____."

9. When someone is leaving on a trip, you say "Bon _____."

Geography Match-Up

Before class, copy and cut apart the capital and country cards. Then, during class, give each student a card. On a signal, have the students move around the room trying to match the countries with their capital cities. The students should not show their cards to each other until they think they have found their correct partners. As the partners find each other, they should move to the front of the room and stand in pairs. When all the students have come to the front of the room, let the pairs read their cards and give the class an opportunity to approve or disapprove the matches. If any pairs are matched incorrectly, the class should work together to correct the matches.

Athens	Greece
Beijing	China
Beirut	Lebanon
Bogotá	Columbia
Cairo	Egypt
Copenhagen	Denmark
Damascus	Syria
Kinshasa	Zaire
Lagos	Nigeria
Lima	Peru

(continued on next page)

Lisbon	Portugal
London	England
Manila	Philippines
Maputo	Mozambique
Moscow	Soviet Union
Nairobi	Kenya
New Delhi	India
Ottawa	Canada
Paris	France
Rome	Italy
Santiago	Chile
Sofia	Bulgaria
Tehran	Iran
Tokyo	Japan
Warsaw	Poland

Geography Crossword Puzzle

Complete this puzzle using the clues below.

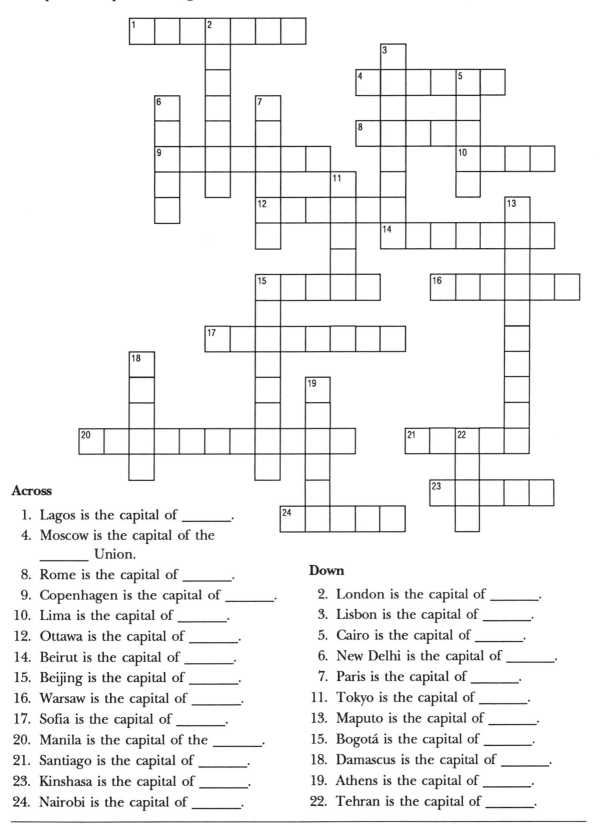

Across

1. Lagos is the capital of _____.
4. Moscow is the capital of the _____ Union.
8. Rome is the capital of _____.
9. Copenhagen is the capital of _____.
10. Lima is the capital of _____.
12. Ottawa is the capital of _____.
14. Beirut is the capital of _____.
15. Beijing is the capital of _____.
16. Warsaw is the capital of _____.
17. Sofia is the capital of _____.
20. Manila is the capital of the _____.
21. Santiago is the capital of _____.
23. Kinshasa is the capital of _____.
24. Nairobi is the capital of _____.

Down

2. London is the capital of _____.
3. Lisbon is the capital of _____.
5. Cairo is the capital of _____.
6. New Delhi is the capital of _____.
7. Paris is the capital of _____.
11. Tokyo is the capital of _____.
13. Maputo is the capital of _____.
15. Bogotá is the capital of _____.
18. Damascus is the capital of _____.
19. Athens is the capital of _____.
22. Tehran is the capital of _____.

Meal Match-Up

Before class, copy and cut apart the word and definition cards. Then, during class, give each student a card. On a signal, have the students move around the room trying to match the words with their definitions. The students should not show their cards to each other until they think they have found their correct partners. As the partners find each other, they should move to the front of the room and stand in pairs. When all the students have come to the front of the room, have the pairs read their cards and give the class an opportunity to approve or disapprove the matches. If any pairs are matched incorrectly, the class should work together to correct the matches. Then instruct the students to get in groups according to the meal at which each food is usually eaten. Go over the groupings the students select and discuss other possible arrangements

bacon	thin strips of salted, smoked pork
breakfast	the morning meal
cake	a sweet food made of flour, oil, eggs, and sugar and baked in an oven
casserole	a hot mixture of meats, vegetables, and/or other foods
chips	very thin pieces of fried potatoes
dinner	the evening meal
fruit	a part of a bush or tree that can be eaten
hamburger	fried or grilled ground beef on a bun

(continued on next page)

juice	liquid from a fruit or vegetable
lunch	the midday meal
pancake	a flat cake made of thin batter and cooked on both sides
pasta	foods made from flour paste, such as macaroni, spaghetti, and ravioli
pie	fruit or some other filling baked in a pastry shell
pizza	a pastry disk topped with tomato sauce, cheese, and usually meats or vegetables
salad	a mixture of mostly vegetables or fruits, usually served cold
sandwich	two slices of bread with meat or some other food between them
snack	food that is eaten between regular meals
soup	a liquid food made by boiling meat, vegetables, or other foods in water
steak	a slice of beef
toast	bread that is heated until it is brown and crisp

Meal Crossword Puzzle

Complete this puzzle using the clues below.

Across

4. thin strips of salted, smoked pork
5. a part of a bush or tree that can be eaten
6. the midday meal
7. two slices of bread with meat or some other food between them
9. the morning meal
11. most people _____ three meals a day
14. foods made from flour paste, such as macaroni, spaghetti, and ravioli
15. a liquid food made by boiling meat, vegetables, or other foods in water
16. fruit or some other filling baked in a pastry shell
17. a hot mixture of meats, vegetables, and/or other foods
19. a mixture of mostly vegetables or fruits, usually served cold

20. a flat cake made of thin batter and cooked on both sides

Down

1. the evening meal
2. bread that is heated until it is brown and crisp
3. liquid from a fruit or vegetable
8. fried or grilled ground beef on a bun
10. a slice of beef
12. a sweet food made of flour, oil, eggs, and sugar and baked in an oven
13. very thin pieces of fried potatoes
16. a pastry disk topped with tomato sauce, cheese, and usually meats or vegetables
18. food that is eaten between regular meals

Party Un-Mixer

Before class, study the directions in the prompt to be sure you understand the activity. Copy and cut apart the information cards. (**Note:** The party un-mixer is planned for a class of forty students. If you have fewer students, you can easily adapt the activity as follows:

1. Arrange the information cards in the order indicated on page 110.
2. Remove the cards for Amanda and John.
3. Remove additional pairs of cards as needed, moving down the list, until the number of cards remaining is equal to the number of students in your class.
4. On the pair of cards following those you have removed, change the direction lines to read "Stand between Mark and Diana's children and *(the couple on the next pair of cards)*."

If your class has an odd number of students, take a card and play yourself, or have two students share one card.)

At class time, give one card to each student. Read the prompt aloud, answer any questions the students have, and give a signal to begin the activity.

Prompt

Mark and Diana have been married for fifteen years. They are having a big party to celebrate their anniversary. It is a formal dinner with assigned seats. At the beginning of the party, the guests will walk around and find their dinner partners. Then the partners will line up together to go in to dinner. The guests must be careful to line up in the correct order.

Each of you has a card containing the information you need to play the game. The card tells your name for the game. It also tells who your dinner partner is. You must find your partner by talking to your classmates. You cannot ask questions; you can only give information. You can say, for example, "Hello, I'm Hilda. I'm Diana's cousin. I'm looking for Lloyd." Be sure to introduce yourself using the name on your card. You are encouraged to make up information about yourself and exchange small talk with your classmates as you would at a real party.

When you find your partner, you must use the information on your card to get in line for dinner. You will have to talk to your classmates in order to find the correct people to stand between. Work with your partner to find your place in line.

When all the pairs are lined up, you will say your names and I will check to see if you are in the correct order. Are there any questions? (pause) All right, stand up and begin looking for your dinner partners.

You are **Mark**.

You are looking for **Diana**.

You are the **host**.

Stand **at the front of the line**.

You are **Diana**.

You are looking for **Mark**.

You are **the hostess**.

Stand **at the front of the line**.

You are **Linda**.

You are looking for **Phillip**.

You are **Mark's mother**.

Stand between **Mark and Diana** and **Diana's parents**.

You are **Phillip**.

You are looking for **Linda**.

You are **Mark's father**.

Stand between **Mark and Diana** and **Diana's parents**.

You are **Greta**.

You are looking for **George**.

You are **Diana's mother**.

Stand between **Mark's parents** and **Mark's uncle and aunt**.

You are **George**.

You are looking for **Greta**.

You are **Diana's father**.

Stand between **Mark's parents** and **Mark's uncle and aunt**.

You are **Eric**.

You are looking for **Anne**.

You are **Mark's uncle**.

Stand between **Diana's parents** and **Diana's uncle and aunt**.

You are **Anne**.

You are looking for **Eric**.

You are **Mark's aunt**.

Stand between **Diana's parents** and **Diana's uncle and aunt**.

You are **Bianca**.

You are looking for **David**.

You are **Diana's aunt**.

Stand between **Mark's uncle and aunt** and **Mark's brother and sister-in-law**.

You are **David**.

You are looking for **Bianca**.

You are **Diana's uncle**.

Stand between **Mark's uncle and aunt** and **Mark's brother and sister-in-law**.

You are **Andrew**.

You are looking for **Leila**.

You are **Mark's brother**.

Stand between **Diana's uncle and aunt** and **Diana's sister and brother-in-law**.

You are **Leila**.

You are looking for **Andrew**.

You are **Mark's sister-in-law**.

Stand between **Diana's uncle and aunt** and **Diana's sister and brother-in-law**.

You are **Peter**.

You are looking for **Caroline**.

You are **Diana's brother-in-law**.

Stand between **Mark's brother and sister-in-law** and **Diana's best friends**.

You are **Caroline**.

You are looking for **Peter**.

You are **Diana's sister**.

Stand between **Mark's brother and sister-in-law** and **Diana's best friends**.

You are **Terry**.

You are looking for **Marty**.

You are **one of Diana's best friends**.

Stand between **Diana's sister and brother-in-law** and **Mark's school friends**.

You are **Marty**.

You are looking for **Terry**.

You are **one of Diana's best friends**.

Stand between **Diana's sister and brother-in-law** and **Mark's school friends**.

You are **Bill**.

You are looking for **Sue**.

You are **one of Mark's school friends**.

Stand between **Diana's best friends** and **Mark and Diana's children**.

You are **Sue**.

You are looking for **Bill**.

You are **one of Mark's school friends**.

Stand between **Diana's best friends** and **Mark and Diana's children**.

You are **Greg**.

You are looking for **Jennifer**.

You are **Mark and Diana's son**.

Stand between **Mark's school friends** and **Mark's boss and his wife**.

You are **Jennifer**.

You are looking for **Greg**.

You are **Mark and Diana's daughter**.

Stand between **Mark's school friends** and **Mark's boss and his wife**.

You are **Amanda**.

You are looking for **John**.

You are **Mark's boss's wife**.

Stand between **Mark and Diana's children** and **Diana's boss and her husband**.

You are **John**.

You are looking for **Amanda**.

You are **Mark's boss**.

Stand between **Mark and Diana's children** and **Diana's boss and her husband**.

You are **Benjamin**.

You are looking for **Stephanie**.

You are **Diana's boss's husband**.

Stand between **Mark's boss and his wife** and **Diana's cousin and her husband**.

You are **Stephanie**.

You are looking for **Benjamin**.

You are **Diana's boss**.

Stand between **Mark's boss and his wife** and **Diana's cousin and her husband**.

You are **Hilda**.

You are looking for **Lloyd**.

You are **Diana's cousin**.

Stand between **Diana's boss and her husband** and **Mark's doctor and her husband**.

You are **Lloyd**.

You are looking for **Hilda**.

You are **Diana's cousin's husband**.

Stand between **Diana's boss and her husband** and **Mark's doctor and her husband**.

You are **Maria**.

You are looking for **Carlos**.

You are **Mark's doctor**.

Stand between **Diana's cousin and her husband** and **Mark's best friends**.

You are **Carlos**.

You are looking for **Maria**.

You are **Mark's doctor's husband**.

Stand between **Diana's cousin and her husband** and **Mark's best friends**.

You are **Kathy**.

You are looking for **Larry**.

You are **one of Mark's best friends**.

Stand between **Mark's doctor and her husband** and **Diana's teacher and his wife**.

You are **Larry**.

You are looking for **Kathy**.

You are **one of Mark's best friends**.

Stand between **Mark's doctor and her husband** and **Diana's teacher and his wife**.

You are **Ken**.

You are looking for **Joan**.

You are **Diana's teacher**.

Stand between **Mark's best friends** and **Mark's teacher and her husband**.

You are **Joan**.

You are looking for **Ken**.

You are **Diana's teacher's wife**.

Stand between **Mark's best friends** and **Mark's teacher and her husband**.

You are **Howard**.

You are looking for **Sylvia**.

You are **Mark's teacher's husband**.

Stand between **Diana's teacher and his wife** and **Mark's cousin and his wife**.

You are **Sylvia**.

You are looking for **Howard**.

You are **Mark's teacher**.

Stand between **Diana's teacher and his wife** and **Mark's cousin and his wife**.

You are **Robert**.

You are looking for **Alice**.

You are **Mark's cousin**.

Stand between **Mark's teacher and her husband** and **Mark and Diana's neighbors**.

You are **Alice**.

You are looking for **Robert**.

You are **Mark's cousin's wife**.

Stand between **Mark's teacher and her husband** and **Mark and Diana's neighbors**.

You are **Steve**.

You are looking for **Maureen**.

You are **Mark and Diana's neighbor**.

Stand between **Mark's cousin and his wife** and **Mark's parents' best friends**.

You are **Maureen**.

You are looking for **Steve**.

You are **Mark and Diana's neighbor**.

Stand between **Mark's cousin and his wife** and **Mark's parents' best friends**.

You are **Jeff**.

You are looking for **Julie**.

You are **Mark's parents' best friends**.

Stand **at the end of the line**.

You are **Julie**.

You are looking for **Jeff**.

You are **Mark's parents' best friends**.

Stand **at the end of the line**.

Correct Line-Up for Party Un-Mixer

1. Mark and Diana
2. Linda and Phillip
3. George and Greta
4. Eric and Anne
5. Bianca and David
6. Andrew and Leila
7. Peter and Caroline
8. Terry and Marty
9. Bill and Sue
10. Greg and Jennifer
11. Amanda and John
12. Benjamin and Stephanie
13. Hilda and Lloyd
14. Carlos and Maria
15. Kathy and Larry
16. Ken and Joan
17. Howard and Sylvia
18. Robert and Alice
19. Steve and Maureen
20. Jeff and Julie

Dicto-Pictures

Before class, select one of the six pictures to use in a warm-up activity with the whole class. Then select at least two of the remaining pictures to distribute to the students. Make enough copies for each student to have one picture.

For your warm-up activity, make sure each student has a blank piece of paper and a pencil. Explain that you will describe a picture that is made up of simple geometric shapes. As they listen to your description, the students must draw the picture on their paper. Your directions will sound something like this: "Draw a circle in the center of the page. Above the circle draw a small square. In the center of the circle draw a triangle." When you're finished describing the picture, show it to the class. Have the students show their pictures and compare them to the original. Discuss some guidelines for giving and following directions.

Next, pair the students and give each student a picture, making sure the partners have different pictures. Without showing each other their pictures, the partners must take turns describing their pictures for the other person to draw on a blank piece of paper. After each student has finished describing his or her picture, the partners should compare the dictated picture to the original.

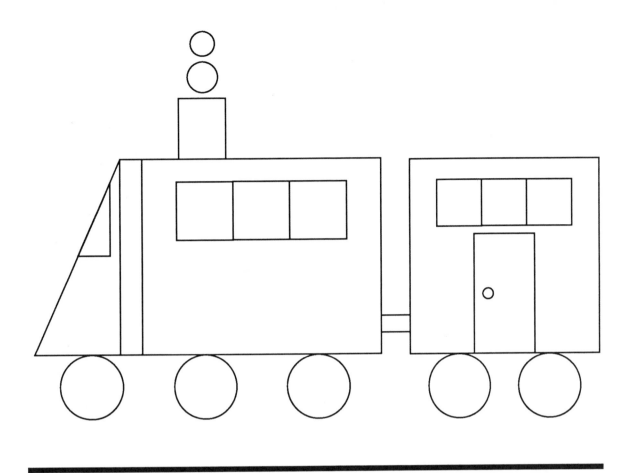

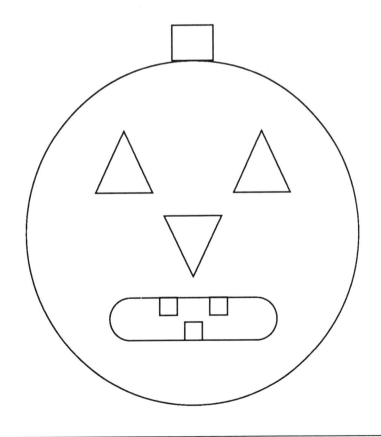

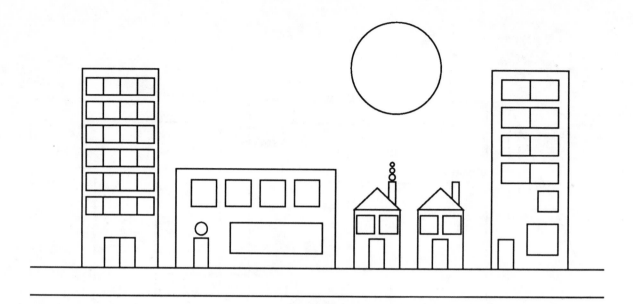

114

Part

3

Jigsaw
Activities

Making a Family Budget

Directions to the Teacher

This can be a one-day or a multiple-day project for your class.

To begin, the class must be divided into "families." Each family should have five members. You may choose the families at random, allow the students to choose their own groups, or use any other means of group selection. It is recommended, however, that you choose the families carefully, since they may be working together for up to a week. It's wise to group students with different levels of language ability. Try to include one strong student in each family.

The first task for the students is to select family names. The groups will be referred to by their family names during the entire exercise.

Next, the students need to establish the relationships in their families. As in real life, a family may be made up of all females or all males. The students must decide who their family members are. They may create any set of relationships they desire. Each family then must choose an adult family member to be the family head. The family head will speak for the family throughout the exercise. You will address the family heads only, and they will communicate with the rest of their families. When it is time to report on the family budgets, the family heads will speak for their families.

The first round begins when you give each family head a piece of paper and a pencil and directions for the following task. The members of each family must take turns writing down one thing on which a family should spend money during a month. The family members pass the paper around their circle as often as necessary until they cannot think of any more items to add to the list.

This may conclude your first day's activities. If it does, collect the lists from each family so you can hand them out again the next day. Make sure the family name is written on each list.

Ask the family heads how many items are on their lists. Have the head of the family with the longest list write that list on the chalkboard. Ask the other families to compare their lists with the list on the board to see if any of the items on their lists are missing from the list on the board. Add all omitted items to the board list. Any member of any family may now challenge anything on the board list. By class consensus, an item can be removed. The final list becomes the master list for each family.

The items on the board now must be reviewed by each family. The first task for each family is to decide which of the items are necessities; that is, items that the family **must** have. A second round of family discussions will focus on those items that are important to the family, although not truly essential. These are the family needs. A third round of discussion focuses on those items that the family wants, but may be able to do without.

In the end, each family should have three lists: one of **necessities**, one of **needs**, and one of **wants**. The family heads now put their lists on the board. The lists from the various families may be different, which could lead to a class discussion of how family values are similar and how they differ.

This may conclude your second day's activities. If it does, collect the three lists from each family. These lists will not be needed for the next day's activities.

The class is now ready to participate in the Family Budget cooperative activity. Please note: *It is not necessary for the class to participate in the first two days' activities in order to do the Family Budget. The activity may be started at this point by selecting and naming the families and choosing family heads.*

Before class, make five copies of pages 119–121 to distribute to the five families. Put together the income card and expense cards for each family by cutting apart the six sections of page 120 and folding each one in half to make a two-sided card. Tape the open sides of the cards together.

At class time, give each family head a set of the six prepared cards, one copy of the student directions, and a copy of the check register. Allow the students to work in groups on the activity. The family members should consult each other about what to do before they ask you any questions. You must respond only to the family heads, and your first response should always be, "Have you discussed this with your family yet?" Only if the answer is yes should you assist in solving the problem. If the family has not yet discussed the problem, they should be directed to try to resolve it for themselves. Only as a last resort should you become involved.

Since all of the families start with the same amount of money and have the same spending demands, the activity ends when each family is satisfied that it has spent its money wisely. The family heads then report to the class the amount of money their families have left at the end of the month. Encourage a class discussion to discover how each family came up with a different spending pattern.

Student Directions for Making a Family Budget

Your family needs to make a budget for this month. You must work together to make decisions and solve any problems. Place your income card in the middle of the family. This card tells how much money your family has for the whole month. Give each family member a numbered expenses card.

Look carefully at your expenses card. It includes three kinds of expenses.

Necessities: things your family must pay for each month
Needs: things that are important to your family
Wants: things you want but may be able to live without

You may not **show** your card to anybody. You may **tell** your family members what your card says.

With your family, decide what you will do with your money for the month. You have enough money to buy many things, but you can't buy everything.

When you have decided what you will buy, use the check register to record each amount you spend. You cannot spend more money than you have in the bank. Any money you do not spend will be considered savings for the future. When all the families are finished, your family head must report on your budget to the class.

Income and Expenses Cards

Necessity: rent, $500
    Need: new clothes to attend a wedding, $175
    Want: tickets to a rock concert, $50
	Person 1

Necessity: food, $400
    Need: new seat covers for your old car, $150
    Want: a compact disc player for your stereo system, $250
	Person 2

Necessity: bills from department stores and gasoline companies, $250
    Need: dinner out with the family to celebrate your birthday, $100
    Want: Compact discs, $125
	Person 3

Necessity: insurance payments, $300
    Need: savings for college, $100
    Want: new party shoes, $120
	Person 4

Necessity: utilities, $135
    Need: savings for next year's vacation, $100
    Want: a camera to photograph the family, $175
	Person 5

$2,500	Income Card

Check Register

Check No.	Date	Transaction	Payment	Deposit	Balance
					$2,500

Going to Treasure Island

Directions to the Teacher

For this activity, the class should be divided into groups of four. Each group may choose a name for itself. The name of a ship would be appropriate. Give each group the following items:

- one copy of the student directions
- one set of ten applications
- one crew list

Instruct the group members to work together to select a crew of six for their ship. After each group has selected a crew and recorded it on the crew list, have each group put its crew list on the board. Encourage a class discussion of the similarities and differences between the crews and the reasons for each group's decisions.

Be sure to point out that there is not a single correct answer for this activity, and that each group's choices are valid.

Student Directions for Going to Treasure Island

You have found a real treasure map. According to the map, many years ago a pirate buried a large amount of money and gold in a big box on a faraway island. Your group of four people is planning to buy a ship and go looking for the treasure, but first you must choose six more people for your ship's crew. You have applications from ten people who want to go with you to look for the treasure.

You paid a private detective to give you information about the ten applicants. The detective wrote some information at the bottom of each application.

Read each application carefully with your group. Notice that there are some positive things and some negative things about each of the applicants. After studying all the applications, work together to choose your six crew members.

After you've decided on your crew members, record their names and the names of your group members on your crew list. Write down what each of the six people you chose will do to help find the treasure.

When all the groups are finished, you will write your crew list on the board and compare it to the other groups' crew lists. Be prepared to discuss the reasons for your choices.

Crew List

Group Member _____

Group Member _____

Group Member _____

Group Member _____

Other Crew Members

1. _____ job _____

2. _____ job _____

3. _____ job _____

4. _____ job _____

5. _____ job _____

6. _____ job _____

APPLICATION

NAME OF APPLICANT <u>Jennifer Waters</u>

ADDRESS <u>9624 Wharfside St.</u>
<u>Blue Island, Washington</u>

AGE <u>22</u>   OCCUPATION <u>factory worker</u>

MEMBERS OF YOUR FAMILY

NAME <u>Brian</u>   RELATION <u>husband</u>   AGE <u>25</u>

NAME <u>Teddy</u>   RELATION <u>son</u>   AGE <u>3 mo.</u>

NAME _____   RELATION _____   AGE _____

NAME _____   RELATION _____   AGE _____

WHAT CAN YOU DO TO HELP FIND THE TREASURE?

I am very strong and a good worker. I can help by working long hours at hard work. I have worked on ships before.

DETECTIVE AGENCY REPORT

Jennifer loves her husband. She talks a lot about her new baby.

APPLICATION

NAME OF APPLICANT __Greg Franklin__

ADDRESS __1200 Dos St.__

__Detroit, Michigan__

AGE __20__   OCCUPATION __mechanic__

MEMBERS OF YOUR FAMILY

NAME __none__ _____ RELATION _____ AGE _____

NAME _____ RELATION _____ AGE _____

NAME _____ RELATION _____ AGE _____

NAME _____ RELATION _____ AGE _____

WHAT CAN YOU DO TO HELP FIND THE TREASURE?

I can fix motors very well. I can make any motor work.

DETECTIVE AGENCY REPORT

Greg has a lot of trouble working with people. He gets into a lot of fights.

APPLICATION

NAME OF APPLICANT _MARK O'REEM_

ADDRESS _2047 OVERVIEW ST._
REDONDO BEACH, CALIFORNIA

AGE _40_   OCCUPATION _BOOKKEEPER_

MEMBERS OF YOUR FAMILY

NAME _TRICIA_   RELATION _WIFE_   AGE _38_

NAME _____   RELATION _____   AGE _____

NAME _____   RELATION _____   AGE _____

NAME _____   RELATION _____   AGE _____

WHAT CAN YOU DO TO HELP FIND THE TREASURE?

I KNOW HOW TO SAVE MONEY AND BUY THINGS
CHEAPLY. I CAN KEEP THE COSTS LOW AND
KEEP GOOD RECORDS.

DETECTIVE AGENCY REPORT

Mark was fired from his last job because
his boss thought he stole money from
the company.

APPLICATION

NAME OF APPLICANT Pam Friedman

ADDRESS 92 Western View Ave.

Maui, Hawaii

AGE 55   OCCUPATION social worker

MEMBERS OF YOUR FAMILY

NAME Dick   RELATION husband   AGE 50

NAME Claire   RELATION mother   AGE 82

NAME Herman   RELATION father   AGE 89

NAME _____   RELATION _____   AGE _____

WHAT CAN YOU DO TO HELP FIND THE TREASURE?

I can help all the crew members get along well.
I can help the people work together.

DETECTIVE AGENCY REPORT

Some people think Pam is too nosy.
She asks a lot of personal questions
about people.

APPLICATION

NAME OF APPLICANT _Leo Karlin_

ADDRESS _12 W. 3rd St._

Anchorage, Alaska

AGE _34_   OCCUPATION _carpenter_

MEMBERS OF YOUR FAMILY

NAME _Shirley_   RELATION _wife_   AGE _32_

NAME _Fred_   RELATION _son_   AGE _14_

NAME _Ellen_   RELATION _daughter_   AGE _12_

NAME _____   RELATION _____   AGE _____

WHAT CAN YOU DO TO HELP FIND THE TREASURE?

I can fix and make anything out of wood.
I am also good with metal. I can help fix
the boat.

DETECTIVE AGENCY REPORT

Leo learned to work with wood and metal
while he was in jail.

APPLICATION

NAME OF APPLICANT Stephanie Chiprin

ADDRESS 2961 Jeff St.

Hollywood, California

AGE 18   OCCUPATION salesperson (part-time)

MEMBERS OF YOUR FAMILY

NAME none _____ RELATION _____ AGE _____

NAME _____ RELATION _____ AGE _____

NAME _____ RELATION _____ AGE _____

NAME _____ RELATION _____ AGE _____

WHAT CAN YOU DO TO HELP FIND THE TREASURE?

I hope to use the money I make to help poor and homeless people in my city.

DETECTIVE AGENCY REPORT

Stephanie just graduated from high school. She has never had a full-time job.

APPLICATION

NAME OF APPLICANT _Arthur Gorlick_

ADDRESS _1285 Hearst St._

Seattle, Washington

AGE _45_   OCCUPATION _reporter_

MEMBERS OF YOUR FAMILY

NAME _Lynne_   RELATION _wife_   AGE _44_

NAME _Peter_   RELATION _son_   AGE _22_

NAME _Karen_   RELATION _daughter_   AGE _20_

NAME _Lisa_   RELATION _daughter_   AGE _18_

WHAT CAN YOU DO TO HELP FIND THE TREASURE?

I can keep good records of the trip. After we
return, I can write a book about what
happened on the trip.

//

DETECTIVE AGENCY REPORT

Arthur is a very nice person. Sometimes
he doesn't like to work hard.

APPLICATION

NAME OF APPLICANT _Juan Mendoza_

ADDRESS _451 Soto St._

Los Angeles, California

AGE _67_   OCCUPATION _retired math teacher_

MEMBERS OF YOUR FAMILY

NAME _Lois_   RELATION _wife_   AGE _deceased_

NAME _Tomas_   RELATION _son_   AGE _32 (married)_

NAME _Anna_   RELATION _daughter_   AGE _30 (married)_

NAME _____   RELATION _____ AGE _____

WHAT CAN YOU DO TO HELP FIND THE TREASURE?

With my knowledge of math, I can help navigate the ship.

DETECTIVE AGENCY REPORT

Juan was a respected math teacher. He retired two years ago. Some of his former students say he was bossy and not a nice person.

APPLICATION

NAME OF APPLICANT __Mary Winslow__

ADDRESS __219 Elm Street__

__San Diego, California__

AGE __34__   OCCUPATION __police captain__

MEMBERS OF YOUR FAMILY

NAME __Don__ RELATION __husband__ AGE __34__

NAME __Martin__ RELATION __son__ AGE __14__

NAME _____ RELATION _____ AGE _____

NAME _____ RELATION _____ AGE _____

WHAT CAN YOU DO TO HELP FIND THE TREASURE?

As a police officer, I am a good leader.
People listen to me and do what I tell them
to do even if they don't want to.

DETECTIVE AGENCY REPORT

Mary is a respected police officer. She
had a heart attack two years ago.

APPLICATION

NAME OF APPLICANT <u>John Argent</u>
ADDRESS <u>24 Mermaid Street</u>
<u>Kudat, North Borneo, Malaysia</u>
AGE <u>47</u> OCCUPATION <u>cook/sailor</u>

MEMBERS OF YOUR FAMILY

NAME <u>none</u> RELATION _____ AGE _____
NAME _____ RELATION _____ AGE _____
NAME _____ RELATION _____ AGE _____
NAME _____ RELATION _____ AGE _____

WHAT CAN YOU DO TO HELP FIND THE TREASURE?

<u>I know the ocean and can cook. I know</u>
<u>a lot about pirates.</u>

DETECTIVE AGENCY REPORT

<u>John has a wooden leg. He is a good</u>
<u>cook. Some people say he cannot be</u>
<u>trusted. He knows some real pirates.</u>

Lower Wages for Youths

Directions to the Teacher

This activity takes the form of a controlled debate. Each cooperative learning group must prepare to discuss both sides of an issue. The issue in this activity is setting a lower minimum wage for young people. However, any issue that appeals to your class may be used for a controlled debate. The issues could come from the newspaper or from school activities.

Before asking the students to work in their groups, lead a class discussion of some of the vocabulary that may be needed during the activity. You may wish to review or teach some or all of the following terms:

wages	working conditions
salary	labor law
employ	bad practice
adult	part time
substitute	career ladder
fire	entry level
unfair	take advantage of
encourage	unfair competition

Divide the class into groups of four. Give each group a copy of the student directions and a copy of the list of arguments. Instruct the groups to begin making their lists. As the students work, circulate among the groups so you can supply in writing any vocabulary a group may need to express its ideas. Before writing a word or phrase for a group, make sure that none of the group members can provide the needed word(s).

Give the students time to complete and discuss both lists of arguments. Then call on a member of one group to argue one side of the issue. Call on a member of another group to argue the opposite side. Continue until someone from every group has argued for or against the issue. Then let the class vote on the issue. Did the debate help to form or change the students' opinions? Have them discuss which arguments influenced them the most.

A controlled debate such as this one gives students new to the debate process the opportunity to participate because it uses the strength of a cooperative learning group to develop ideas. This activity also helps students to see that there can be valid arguments on both sides of an issue.

Student Directions for Lower Wages for Youths

Many people think it's a good idea for young people to work. Some young people work after school. Others work when they have vacation time. However, young people have trouble finding jobs. Every worker must be paid at least the minimum wage, but some employers think that the minimum wage is too much money to pay young workers.

One idea is to set a special minimum wage for young workers. This wage would be lower than the minimum wage for adult workers.

There are some reasons why setting a lower wage for young workers might be good. There are some reasons why setting a lower wage for young workers might be bad. Your group's first job is to think of these reasons.

Pass the list of arguments around your group. Each time the paper gets to you, add one item to the list. If you can't think of an item, ask the rest of the group for help. You can help the others in your group, too.

First, make a list of arguments **for** a lower minimum wage under the heading "Why a lower wage is a good idea." Your group should write as many ideas as it can. Then make a list of arguments **against** a lower minimum wage under the heading "Why a lower wage is a bad idea." Your group should write as many ideas as it can.

Next, talk about the ideas. Choose the strongest arguments for each side of the issue. Make sure that every member of your group can argue for each side of the issue.

Your teacher will ask somebody from your group to argue one side of the issue in front of the class. Then you will all have a chance to vote on the issue and discuss your opinions.

List of Arguments

Should we lower the minimum wage for young people?

Why a lower wage is a good idea

_____
_____
_____
_____
_____
_____
_____
_____
_____
_____
_____
_____
_____
_____
_____
_____
_____
_____
_____
_____

Why a lower wage is a bad idea

_____
_____
_____
_____
_____
_____
_____
_____
_____
_____
_____
_____
_____
_____
_____
_____
_____
_____
_____
_____

Reporting a Crime

Directions to the Teacher

This activity takes the form of a controlled debate. Each cooperative learning group must prepare to discuss both sides of an issue. The issue in this activity is reporting a bully to the teacher. However, any issue that appeals to your class may be used for a controlled debate.

Before asking the students to work in their groups, lead a class discussion of some of the vocabulary that may be needed during the activity. You may wish to review or teach some or all of the following terms:

would	cooperation
could	alone
should	adult
might	get in trouble
bully	leave someone alone
report	help each other
assistance	get help
fight	

Divide the class into groups of four. Give each group a copy of the student directions and a copy of the list of arguments. Instruct the groups to begin making their lists. As the students work, circulate among the groups so you can supply in writing any vocabulary a group may need to express its ideas. Before writing a word or phrase for a group, make sure that none of the group members can provide the needed word(s).

Give the students time to complete and discuss both lists of arguments. Then call on a member of one group to argue one side of the issue. Call on a member of another group to argue the opposite side. Continue until someone from every group has argued for or against the issue. Then let the class vote on the issue. Did the debate help to form or change the students' opinions? Have them discuss which arguments influenced them the most.

A controlled debate such as this one gives students new to the debate process the opportunity to participate because it uses the strength of a cooperative learning group to develop ideas. This activity also helps students to see that there can be valid arguments on both sides of an issue.

Student Directions for Reporting a Crime

A student was walking to school one day. A bully and some of his friends stopped the student. The bully touched the student's pocket to see if he had any change.

"I want your money," said the bully. "If you don't give it to me, my friends and I will beat you up."

The student was afraid, so he gave his money to the bully and his friends. The bully said, "If you tell anybody we took your money, we'll beat you up after school."

This happened three days in a row. Each time, the group of boys took the student's lunch money.

On the third day, the student saw the bully on the school playground. He also saw one of the teachers. He wanted to tell the teacher about what the boys did to him, but he did not know if he should.

Your group's first job is to think of reasons why the student should tell the teacher and reasons why he should not.

Pass the list of arguments around your group. Each time the paper gets to you, add one item to the list. If you can't think of an item, ask the rest of the group for help. You can help the others in your group, too.

First, make a list of arguments **for** telling the teacher under the heading "Why the student should tell the teacher." Your group should write as many ideas as it can. Then make a list of arguments **against** telling the teacher under the heading "Why the student should not tell the teacher." Your group should write as many ideas as it can.

Next, talk about the ideas. Choose the strongest arguments for each side of the issue. Make sure that every member of your group can argue for each side of the issue.

Your teacher will ask somebody from your group to argue one side of the issue in front of the class. Then you will all have a chance to vote on the issue and discuss your opinions.

List of Arguments

Should the student tell the teacher about the bully?

Why the student should tell the teacher	Why the student should not tell the teacher
_____	_____
_____	_____
_____	_____
_____	_____
_____	_____
_____	_____
_____	_____
_____	_____
_____	_____
_____	_____
_____	_____
_____	_____
_____	_____
_____	_____
_____	_____

Building a Family Tree

Directions to the Teacher

This activity will help your students use their reading skills as well as their cognitive abilities. Divide the class into cooperative learning groups of four or eight. Distribute the following materials to each group:

- one copy of the student directions
- one set of eight letters
- one copy of the blank family tree

If the groups are made up of eight members, each person will get one letter. If the groups are made up of four members, each person will get two letters.

Tell the students to read the direction sheet and then begin studying their letters. If a group needs help getting started, tell the members to write everything they know for sure on the family tree. Although the student directions instruct the students not to show their letters to the other members of their group, use discretion in enforcing this rule.

There is only one correct way to group the families. However, the order in which the members of one generation are listed may vary.

After each group has completed its family tree, instruct the group members to make up a story that explains the disappearances of Domingo Fuentes and Alexander Fuentes's family. Then let the groups compare and discuss their family trees and their stories. You may want to have the class vote on the best story.

Student Directions for Building a Family Tree

Mr. Domingo Fuentes has hired your detective agency to locate his son Alexander and Alexander's family. Mr. Fuentes has not heard from his son or his son's family for a few days, and he thinks something is wrong. He went to Alexander's house and found no one at home, but there were eight letters in the mailbox.

Mr. Fuentes sent the letters to your agency in case they contained some clues. He made an appointment to meet with you to provide more information about his son's family. However, Mr. Fuentes did not show up for his appointment. He doesn't answer his telephone or doorbell. He has disappeared, too! Your group must try to find Mr. Fuentes and his son's family.

First, read the letters and use the information they contain to make a complete family tree for Mr. Fuentes's family. Each member of your group should have one or two letters. You may read your letters to the rest of the group, but you cannot show them to anybody in your group. You may ask questions of anyone in your group.

Next, work with the other members of your group to make up a story that explains the disappearances of Mr. Fuentes and his son's family. When all the groups are finished, you will compare your family tree and story with those created by the rest of the class.

A Family Tree

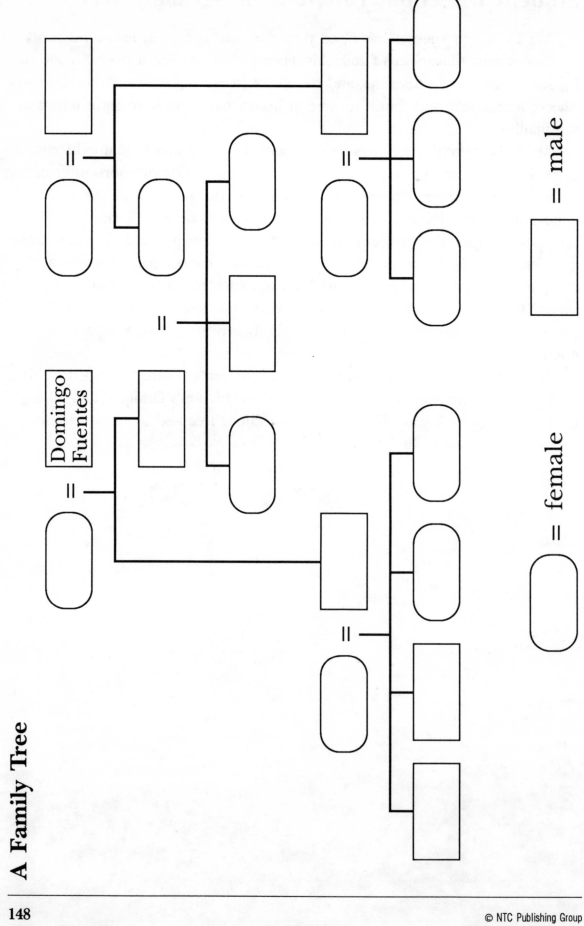

Domingo
Fuentes

= male

= female

First Security Bank

19124 Wilbur Road

Marshall, CA 90004

April 13

Alexander Fuentes
2157 Dell Lane
Marshall, CA 90001

Dear Mr. Fuentes:

As a customer of First Security Bank, you will want to know about our special accounts for college savings for your three children.

College costs increase every year, and the need for a college education grows stronger every year. A college graduate can earn hundreds of thousands of dollars more than a high school graduate in a lifetime. You owe it to your children to send them to a good college, so you must start to save now.

Come in to our friendly bank and let us show you how much money you need to save for college for your children:

Pat	daughter	age 18
Edward	son	age 16
Lois	daughter	age 10

Ask for me or any account officer.

Yours truly,

Dave Dawson

Dave Dawson
Branch Savings Manager

The Bank You Can Trust to Trust in You

Dear Ed,

This is my first chance to write since I started college. Things are going well here, but I miss my friends like you. Your grandmother Mercedes would have liked the Art Center at this college. I hope you will choose to study here when you finish high school.

Your friend,
Tom Harkins

Ed. Fuentes
2157 Dell Lane
Marshall, CA
90001

Storms Department Store

19056 Wilbur Road
Marshall, CA 90004

April 13

Mrs. Alice Fuentes
2157 Dell Lane
Marshall, CA 90001

Dear Mrs. Fuentes:

We at Storms Department Store are sorry that we made an error. Thank you for writing to tell us that we sent the wrong card with a gift you ordered for your niece Evelyn, age 6. We have now sent her the correct gift card. We have also sent to her and her mother, Jane Larkin, a gift certificate for a free lunch at our store's restaurant.

We appreciate your business and hope that we can continue to serve you.

Yours truly,

Ruth Davis

Ruth Davis
Customer Services

A Family Business in a Family Town

Happy Birthday to
our only grandson.

Love,

Grandma Janet
and
Grandpa Carlos

 ———— Message here

On Your Special Day

You're Invited!

What: <u>a Birthday Party for our twins, Sue and Louis</u>

Where: <u>at the Fuentes' house</u>

Date: <u>Sunday, May 12</u>

Time: <u>1:00 to 3:00 P.M.</u>

RSVP: <u>by May 9 to Joan or Tom (555-9446)</u>

Dear Alice,

It really is nice to have a wonderful sister-in-law like you. I am so happy that I married into the Larkin family! Paul and I were thrilled to get the sweater for little Evelyn. She wore it to the free lunch that Storms Department Store sent us. Everybody looked at her. Now her sister Beth wants a sweater just like it. You are so good to all our girls.

All my love,
Jane

Warmest *** ******* Thanks

Message here

🍓 🍓 🍓 🍓 🍓

April 15

Dear Alex,

    Just a quick note because I can't seem to get you on the phone. Would you and your son, Ed, like to join me and my son, Rodney, at a baseball game a week from Saturday? I have tickets for four seats. The boys haven't been together for a while, and cousins should see each other.

    Let me know if you can come. If not, I'll ask Paul and his oldest girl, Maria.

                Your loving brother,
                —Tom

🍓 🍓 🍓 🍓 🍓

Banner High School
Student Council

The Red Tigers

April 10

Pat Fuentes
2157 Dell Lane
Marshall, CA 90001

Dear Pat,

   Your cousin Martha Fuentes suggested that I get in touch with you for a project the Banner High School Student Council is beginning.

   We are forming a tutoring group made up of seniors who have good grades. The group members will tutor any students who need help during lunch and after school for one hour. Your cousin thinks you would be a good tutor in Spanish, English, and geometry.

   If you would like to help us help all the students at Banner High School, please come to an informational meeting on Wednesday, May 2, at lunch time in room 154.

   Hope to see you there.

                              Yours truly,

                              Bob Kaplan

                              Bob Kaplan
                              Senior Class Secretary